AA

# 50 WALKS IN Hampshire & Isle of Wight

50 WALKS OF 2–10 MILES

First published 2001
New edition 2008
Reprinted 2009, 2010 and 2011 (twice)

Researched and written by David Hancock
Field checked and updated 2008 by
David Foster

Series Management: Bookwork Creative Associates
Series Editors: Sandy Draper and Marilynne Lanng
Series Design and Concept: Elizabeth Baldin and Andrew Milne
Picture Research: Liz Stacey
Proofreader: Pamela Stagg
Production: Stephanie Allen
Cartography provided by the Mapping Services Department of AA Publishing

Produced by AA Publishing


Published by AA Publishing (a trading name of AA Media Limited, whose registered office is Fanum House, Basing View, Basingstoke, Hampshire RG21 4EA; registered number 06112600)



A04785

ISBNs: 978-0-7495-6053-9 and 978-0-7495-6391-2 (SS)

A CIP catalogue record for this book is available from the British Library.

The contents of this book are believed correct at the time of printing. Nevertheless, the publishers cannot be held responsible for any errors or omissions or for changes in the details given in this book or for the consequences of any reliance on the information it provides. This does not affect your statutory rights. We have tried to ensure accuracy in this book, but things do change and we would be grateful if readers would advise us of any inaccuracies they may encounter.

We have taken all reasonable steps to ensure that these walks are safe and achievable by walkers with a realistic level of fitness. However, all outdoor activities involve a degree of risk and the publishers accept no responsibility for any injuries caused to readers whilst following these walks. For more advice on walking safely see page 144. The mileage range shown on the front cover is for guidance only – some walks may be less than or exceed these distances.

Some of the walks may appear in other AA books and publications.

Visit AA Publishing at theAA.com/shop

Printed by Printer Trento Srl, Italy

Acknowledgements
The Automobile Association would like to thank the following photographers, companies and picture libraries for their assistance in the preparation of this book.

3 AA/D Forss; 9 AA/A Burton; 16/7 AA/D Croucher; 29 AA/M Moody; 34 AA/M Moody; 47 AA/M Moody ; 49 AA/D Forss; 66/7 AA/T Souter; 86/87 AA/M Moody; 95 AA/M Moody; 96 AA/W Voysey; 138/9 AA/A Burton.

Every effort has been made to trace the copyright holders, and we apologise in advance for any accidental errors. We would be happy to apply the corrections in the following edition of this publication.

*Right: Rockbourne (Walk 37)*

AA

# 50 WALKS IN Hampshire & Isle of Wight

50 WALKS OF 2–10 MILES

# Contents

# Contents



**Rating**

Each walk is rated for its relative difficulty compared to the other walks in this book. Walks marked +++ are likely to be shorter and easier with little total ascent. The hardest walks are marked +++

**Walking in Safety**

For advice and safety tips see page 144.

# Locator Map

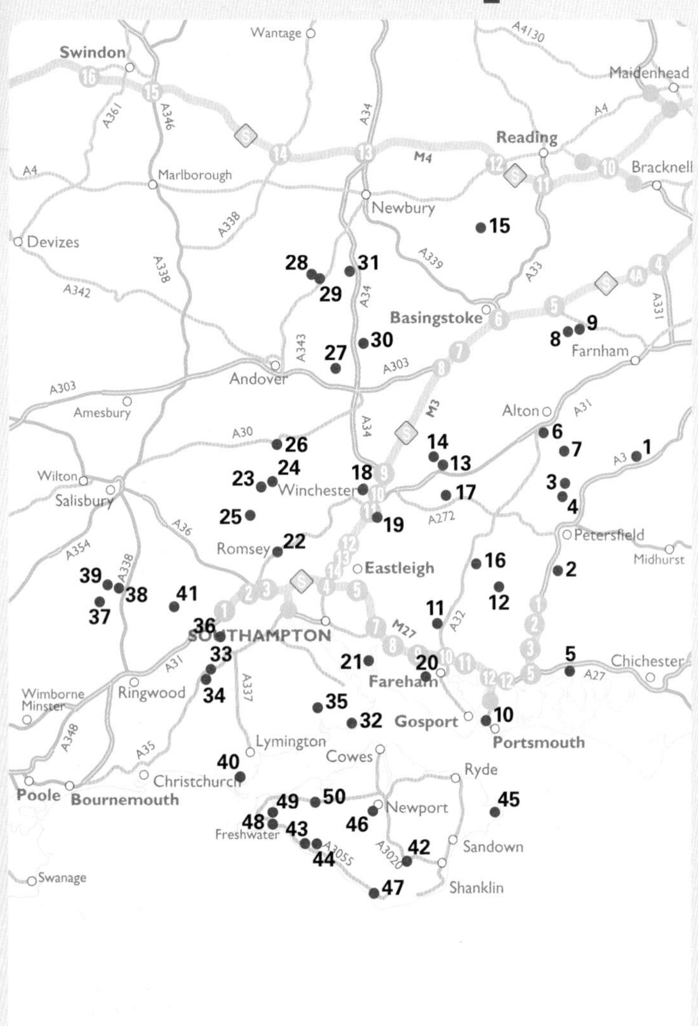


# Legend

| | | | |
|---|---|---|---|
| | Walk Route | | Built-up Area |
| 1 | Route Waypoint | | Woodland Area |
| | Adjoining Path | | Toilet |
| | Viewpoint | P | Car Park |
| • | Place of Interest | | Picnic Area |
| | Steep Section | )( | Bridge |

# Introducing Hampshire & Isle of Wight

Why should you go walking in Hampshire or the Isle of Wight? Walking is enjoyable exercise; it helps maintain fitness and takes you to places no car ever could. And as for Hampshire and the Isle of Wight, they have history in abundance and a diverse and interesting range of landscapes, all linked by an enviable network of over 3,000 miles (4,800km) of rights of way.

You can stride out across the high, rolling, chalk downland of the north Hampshire 'highlands' with far-reaching views, walk through steep, beech-clad 'hangers' close to the Sussex border, or meander along peaceful paths through unspoilt river valleys, etched by the sparkling trout streams of the Test, Itchen, Avon and Meon. Alternatively, you can wander across lonely salt marshes and beside fascinating coastal inlets or, perhaps, explore the beautiful medieval forest and heathland of the New Forest, the jewel in Hampshire's crown. You will find that the county's extensive web of footpaths, bridleways and ancient byways criss-crosses them all. Included among these routes are eight distinctively waymarked long distance paths, including the Avon Valley Path in the west, the Hangers Way in the east, the Wayfarers Walk and Test Way which traverse the county from north to south, and the South Downs Way which terminates in Winchester, the ancient capital of Wessex and England, and Hampshire's county town.

### Unrivalled landscape

Hampshire's varied landscape of hills and heaths, downlands and forests, valleys and coast is without rival in southern England. Combine these varied landscapes and terrains with secluded and idyllic villages, complete with thatched and timber-framed cottages and Norman churches, elegant Georgian market towns, historic ports and cities, restored canals and ancient abbeys, forts and castles, then you have a county that is paradise for the walking fraternity.

**PUBLIC TRANSPORT**

Either the start points of the walks, or villages en route, are within easy reach from public transport. Walks 5, 10, 18/19, 21, 22 and 25 start close to railway stations. For train times call the 24-hour national train information line on 08457 48 49 50. For ferry travel to the Isle of Wight call Wightlink (Portsmouth–Fishbourne or Ryde, Lymington–Yarmouth) on 0871 376 4342 or Red Funnel (Southampton–East Cowes) on 0844 844 9988. You can also get travel information from the national public transport enquiry line on 0871 200 2233 between 8am and 8pm, or look on the internet (www.traveline.info).

Equally appealing and just a short ferry voyage away is the Isle of Wight, an enchanting island with magnificent coastal views, sandy bays, sheltered creeks, picturesque villages and a unique blend of old-world charm. Despite being only 23 miles (37km) long and 13 miles (21km) wide, this diamond-shaped haven offers an amazing variety of scenery and, in addition to 64 miles (105km) of exhilarating coastal paths, has 500 miles (805km) of footpaths and bridleways, including eight inland trails that traverse the island's breezy downland and unspoilt farmland. For two weeks during May, the Isle of Wight Walking Festival draws on the island's special appeal. Among the guided and unguided walks offered are fun walks for the family and challenging hikes for enthusiasts.

The walks in this book are circular and vary in length from 2 miles (3.2km) to 9.5 miles (15.3km). All are rural, except for a stroll around the historic dockland in Old Portsmouth and a city walk that incorporates the celebrated sights and narrow streets of Winchester. Ten of the walks offer shorter or longer options depending on your level of fitness and/or the time you have available. All have been devised with the recreational rambler in mind, so you don't need to be a serious hiker to undertake them.

# Using this book

### INFORMATION PANELS

An information panel for each walk shows its relative difficulty (see page 5), the distance and total amount of ascent. An indication of the gradients you will encounter is shown by the rating ▲▲▲ (no steep slopes) to ▲▲▲ (several very steep slopes).

### MAPS

There are 30 maps, covering 40 of the walks. Some walks have a suggested option in the same area. The information panel for these walks will tell you how much extra walking is involved. On short-cut suggestions the panel will tell you the total distance if you set out from the start of the main walk. Where an option returns to the same point on the main walk, just the distance of the loop is given. Where an option leaves the main walk at one point and returns to it at another, then the distance shown is for the whole walk. The minimum time suggested is for reasonably fit walkers and doesn't allow for stops. Each walk has a suggested map.

### START POINTS

The start of each walk is given as a six-figure grid reference prefixed by two letters indicating which 100km square of the National Grid it refers to. You'll find more information on grid references on most Ordnance Survey maps.

### DOGS

We have tried to give dog owners useful advice about how dog friendly each walk is. Please respect other countryside users. Keep your dog under control, especially around livestock, and obey local bylaws and other dog control notices.

### CAR PARKING

Many of the car parks suggested are public, but occasionally you may find you have to park on the roadside or in a lay-by. Please be considerate when you leave your car, ensuring that access roads or gates are not blocked and that other vehicles can pass safely.



*Right: Bembridge Life Boat pier (Walk 45)*

WALK 1

# Bramshott – Following Flora's Footsteps

*Wild heathland contrasts with a wooded beauty spot in an area loved by Tennyson and the writer Flora Thompson.*

**DISTANCE** *4 miles (6.4km)* **MINIMUM TIME** *2hrs*

**ASCENT/GRADIENT** *295ft (90m)* ▲▲▲ **LEVEL OF DIFFICULTY** +++

**PATHS** *Woodland paths and heathland tracks, 3 stiles*

**LANDSCAPE** *Wooded valley with lakes. Lofty, heather-covered common with far-reaching views*

**SUGGESTED MAP** *OS Explorer 133 Haslemere & Petersfield*

**START / FINISH** *Grid reference: SU 855336*

**DOG FRIENDLINESS** *Vast expanse of heathland where dogs can run free*

**PARKING** *Unsurfaced car park on edge of Bramshott Common*

**PUBLIC TOILETS** *None en route*

Much of the landscape either side of the busy A3 in this peaceful corner of Hampshire is a mini wilderness of bracken and heather-covered commons and deep wooded valleys etched by tiny streams. Surprisingly, this unspoilt area was once the heart of a thriving iron industry, with streams like the Wey and Downwater being dammed to provide power for the great hammers in the 17th-century ironworks. Timber for the furnaces and iron ore were in plentiful supply locally.

## Writers and Poets

The chain of dams and the lovely wooded ponds at Waggoner's Wells were created in 1615 by Henry Hooke, lord of the manor of Bramshott, to supply his iron foundry. Now a famous beauty spot owned by the National Trust, the three beautiful lakes, surrounded by splendid beech woods and home to a wealth of wildlife, are a delight to explore, especially during the autumn when the colours are magnificent. Like the poet Tennyson and the writer Flora Thompson, who loved to stroll beside the pools, you will be immediately charmed by this secluded haven. Tennyson, who rented Grayshott Farm (now Grayshott Hall) in 1867, wrote his famous short ode *Flower in the Crannied Wall* after pulling a flower from one of the crevices at the wishing well you will pass in the valley bottom.

Flora Thompson lived in both Liphook and Grayshott during her 30 years in Hampshire between 1897 and 1927. She often walked to Waggonner's Wells and Bramshott, returning to Grayshott via Ludshott Common. On these long, inspirational country rambles she would observe and assiduously make notes on the wildlife she encountered. Her detailed nature notes reflecting the changing year, and written in semi-fictional style, appeared in her book *The Peverel Papers*. Flora also describes her life in the area and many of its inhabitants with great affection in the collection of essays called *Heatherley*, which was not published until 1979.

Flora says she 'did not often linger by the lakes' on her Sunday walks, but 'climbed at once by a little sandy track to the heath beyond'. Walk this way today, especially on a Sunday in the summer months; the wonderful wooded vale really does attract the crowds. If you are seeking relative solitude, stride on up to the open heath and the deciduous woodland of Ludshott Common. Here, the sandy paths criss-cross a seemingly vast expanse of purple heather and yellow gorse, and the far-reaching wooded views make the strenuous climb well worth the effort. Flora would certainly have seen stonechats, linnets, redpolls and nightingales here, all of which still nest on the margins of the heath, and, like Tennyson, she would have been fascinated by the eerie drumming call of the nightjar, distinctly heard as dusk falls across the heath on a summer evening.

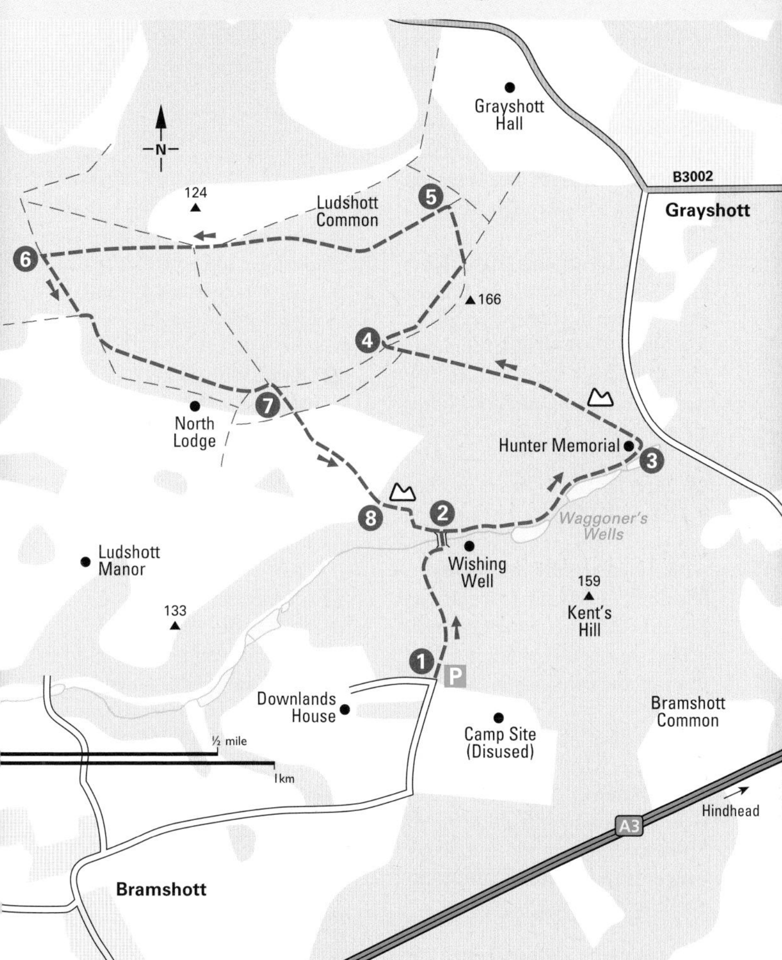


## WALK 1 DIRECTIONS

**1** From the car park, take the defined path beyond the low barrier and gradually descend. At the bottom, take the main bridleway (marked by a blue arrow on a post) that directs you left along a sunken track. Ignore this if it's wet and muddy and climb the path ahead beneath beech trees, then at a fork, keep left down to reach the river and a footbridge.

❷ Cross the bridge and turn right along the footpath parallel with the river. Pass the wishing well and a house and keep to the path through the valley bottom to the left of three ponds, eventually reaching a lane by a ford.

❸ Just before the lane, turn sharp left, pass a memorial stone, and steeply ascend through mixed woodland. As it levels out, cross a path, then a track and soon merge with a wide gravel track. Keep left, pass a bridleway on the left, then, where the track begins to curve left downhill, keep straight on along a path through trees.

❹ Cross a path, then turn right after 50yds (46m) at a broad sandy track bordering lightly wooded heathland. On reaching a junction, fork left across the common. The path soon widens and descends to a T-junction.

❺ Turn left and follow this open heathland trail, edged by bracken and gorse, and eventually merge with a wider sandy trail. Keep left then, on reaching a bench and junction of ways on the common fringe, proceed straight on through the conifer plantation.

❻ At a crossing of paths by a line of electricity poles, turn left with bridleway signs. Bear gently right at a crossways, following the bridleway close to the woodland fringe. Turn left beside electricity poles, and ignore a bridleway turning right. Bear left with the poles; then, after 100yds (91m) turn right at a crossways and broken bridleway sign.

❼ Turn right and keep straight on at the next crossing of routes, following the footpath marker alongside a garden to a stile on the woodland edge. Keep ahead between wire fences to a stile in the field corner.

❽ Steeply descend into woodland to reach a stile. At the track beyond, turn right downhill to the river and footbridge encountered on the outward route. Retrace your steps back to the car park.

### WHERE TO EAT AND DRINK

There are no refreshments available on the route but it makes for an ideal morning, afternoon or summer's evening walk, so why not enjoy a picnic beside one of the three delightful ponds at Waggoner's Wells.

### WHILE YOU'RE THERE

Explore Bramshott Common. Grass covered concrete is all that remains of the huge army camp that stood either side of the A3 during both World Wars. Bramshott Camp or Mudsplosh Camp and Tin Town, a collection of ramshackle huts and shops built of corrugated iron, housed Canadian soldiers and occupied much of the land here. Visit St Mary's churchyard in Bramshott which has a special burial ground containing graves of 350 Canadian soldiers who died during a flu epidemic in 1917.

### WHAT TO LOOK OUT FOR

Look out for the memorial stone dedicated to Sir Robert Hunter, a founder of the National Trust in 1895, who lived in Haslemere. He initiated the local purchase of Hindhead Common before transferring it to the Trust. Walk across Ludshott Common in summer and you may see the dark purplish-brown plummage and the cocked tail of the rare Dartford warbler, and butterflies like the silver-studded blue, grayling and the green hairstreak.

# Butser's Ancient Farm

*Follow shady woodland and glorious downland trails to a unique archaeological farmstead.*



**DISTANCE** *6.75 miles (10.9km)* **MINIMUM TIME** *3hrs*

**ASCENT/GRADIENT** *756ft (230m)* ▲▲▲ **LEVEL OF DIFFICULTY** +++

**PATHS** *Woodland paths, bridleways and forest tracks, 3 stiles*

**LANDSCAPE** *Downland forest and farmland*

**SUGGESTED MAP** *OS Explorer 120 Chichester*

**START / FINISH** *Grid reference: SU 718185*

**DOG FRIENDLINESS** *Dogs can run free in Queen Elizabeth Forest*

**PARKING** *Large pay-and-display car park at country park*

**PUBLIC TOILETS** *Adjacent to visitor centre*

Queen Elizabeth Country Park lies at the western end of the South Downs and forms part of the East Hampshire Area of Outstanding Natural Beauty. Covering some 1,400 acres (567ha), it is dominated by three hills, the chalk downland of Butser Hill, which at 810ft (270m) is Hampshire's second highest point, and the woodland of Holt Down and War Down. Planted with beech and conifer trees in the 1930s, the woodland is commercially managed and provides excellent recreational facilities.

Along with its informative visitor centre and café, it also provides a useful starting point for longer circular walks and more adventurous hikes along the South Downs Way, the Hangers Way or the Staunton Way. Although your walk makes good use of the country park trails, the emphasis is on exploring the Ancient Archaeological Farm south of the park and two of Hampshire's oldest and most scenic villages, Chalton and Buriton.

Allow time to visit the Ancient Farm (open Easter–October) near Chalton. Neither a museum nor a theme park, it is an open-air laboratory for archaeology, focusing on the Iron Age (1000 BC–AD 43) and the Roman period (AD 43– AD 400). Through evidence collected from excavations of prehistoric and Roman sites, it has been possible to recreate a full-scale Iron Age settlement using only the materials and tools that ancient people would have had at their disposal. You can wander around earthworks, view inside a Roman villa with a working hypocaust, see the thatched roundhouses and watch demonstrations of iron smelting, pottery making and weaving. Fields are also being cultivated with ancient crops using replica tools, and animals can be seen in the livestock enclosures. You'll find the settlement particularly atmospheric on a quiet day.

Welcome refreshment can be sought along the lane in Chalton at the impressive, thatched and timbered Red Lion Inn, reputedly the oldest pub in Hampshire. Visit St Michael's Church opposite and you will see a fine 15th-century font and, from the top corner of the churchyard, a memorable downland view. Next comes Buriton, well worth exploring before you climb back to the country park. There's a green with a duck pond, attractive cottages, a large church, rectory and manor house.

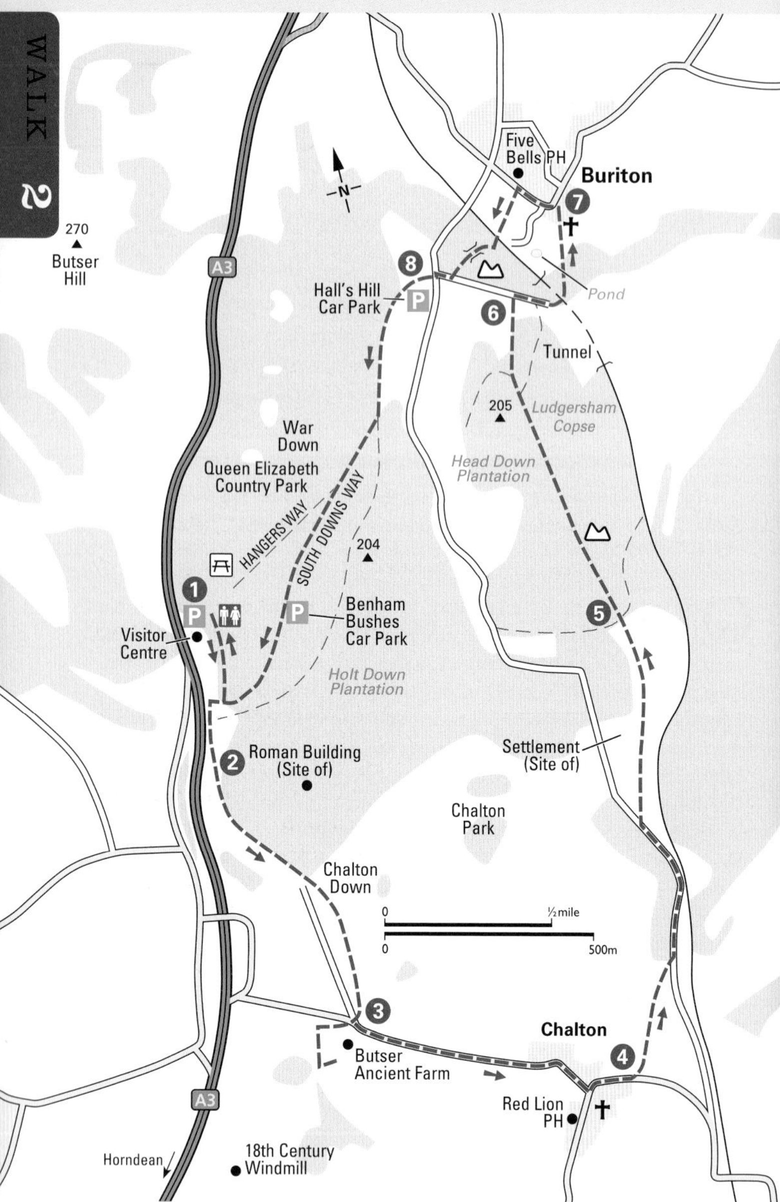


## WALK 2 DIRECTIONS

❶ From the car park, follow the Woodland Trail (green-booted posts) to the right. On reaching the road, turn right then left and join the gravelled track at a blue-topped horseshoe post. Follow the waymarked bridleway past the maintenance yard, and bear away from the A3 on to a grassy lane.

❷ Gently climb between fields, the bridleway soon curving left around woodland, then gradually bear right between fields, noting the 18th-century windmill on the skyline to your right.

3 At the road, turn right to visit Butser Ancient Farm, otherwise turn left and follow the road (some blind bends) for 0.5 mile (800m) into Chalton. Turn left at the junction, signed 'Ditcham'. (Bear right for the Red Lion.)

4 Shortly, at a fork, bear left along a byway. Continue between fields and soon descend through trees to join a road. Turn left, walking parallel to the railway for 0.25 mile (400m), to a stile on the right. Bear half-left across a large field, pass under electricity lines, and enter woodland.

5 At a junction of paths continue straight ahead and steadily climb a wide forest track. On the descent fork left, then almost immediately fork right, down a narrow sunken footpath and continue down to a road (also the South Downs Way).

6 Turn right then, in 100yds (91m), take the footpath left and head steeply down through the trees to a stile. Bear half right across a field to a stile by a gate then follow the path round to the left, passing a pond, into Buriton.

7 Turn left along the High Street then, beside Chapel Cottage, take the footpath left. Go round the village hall and continue past the play area to a gate. Very carefully cross the railway line, go through a gate and keep ahead to a junction with a bridleway. Turn right and steeply ascend to the road. Cross into Hall's Hill car park.

**WHERE TO EAT AND DRINK**

Besides the café in the country park, there is the Red Lion at Chalton, offering Fullers ales and good views from the rear garden, and the Five Bells in Buriton which offers an extensive menu.

**WHAT TO LOOK OUT FOR**

Make a point of visiting the Norman Church of St Mary in Buriton. The 18th-century historian, Edward Gibbon, best known for his book The Decline and Fall of the Roman Empire, lived in the adjacent manor house and is buried in the churchyard. You will also find a memorial window to John Goodyer (1592–1664), one of the first great botanists, who wrote about potatoes and tobacco after they were brought back to this country.

8 Go through a gate and up a wide track (South Downs Way) back into Queen Elizabeth Country Park. Gradually ascend then, just after a track merges from the right, fork right (signed 'South Downs Way walkers and cyclists'). Keep ahead at the barbecue shelter, and descend past a barrier. Pass through Benham Bushes car park, follow a short stretch of metalled road then bear off left with the South Downs Way. Rejoin the road at Gravel Hill car park and turn right, signed 'Hangers Way', and retrace your outward route to the car park.

*Overleaf: Queen Elizabeth Country Park (Walk 2)*

# Looking for Edward Thomas

*Explore the beech-clad hills and vales that so inspired Hamsphire's great poet.*

**DISTANCE** *3 miles (4.8km)* **MINIMUM TIME** *2hrs*

**ASCENT/GRADIENT** *682ft (208m)* ▲▲▲ **LEVEL OF DIFFICULTY** +++

**PATHS** *Field and woodland paths, rutted, wet and muddy tracks (in winter) and short stretches of road, 21 stiles*

**LANDSCAPE** *Rolling, beech-clad hills, a hidden, flower-filled valley and undulating farmland*

**SUGGESTED MAP** *OS Explorer 133 Haslemere & Petersfield*

**START / FINISH** *Grid reference: SU 746291*

**DOG FRIENDLINESS** *Dogs to be kept under control at all times*

**PARKING** *By village green and church in Hawkley*

**PUBLIC TOILETS** *None; outdoor toilets opposite Harrow Inn accessible*

William Cobbett wrote 'beautiful beyond description' in his *Rural Rides*, after passing through Hawkley in 1822, on his way from East Meon to Thursley. In common with other famous literary people who once lived in and wrote about this area, such as naturalist Gilbert White (see Walk 7) and poet Edward Thomas, Cobbett was enchanted by the rolling, beech-clad hills that characterise this relatively unexplored part of Hampshire.

## Abiding Love

Known locally as 'hangers', from the Anglo-Saxon hangra meaning 'sloping wood', these fine beech woods cling to the steep chalk escarpment that links Selborne to Steep. Many have charming names such as Happersnapper Hanger and Strawberry Hanger. Edward Thomas lived at Steep from 1906 to his death in the First World War in 1917. His abiding love for the beech hangers, mysterious combes and the sheer beauty of the landscape inspired him to write some of his finest poems, including *Up in the Wind*, *The New House and Wind* and *Mist*. You, too, will find the views breathtaking as you dip and climb through the hangers to the summit of Shoulder of Mutton Hill, Thomas's favoured spot above his beloved Steep.

The walk begins from Hawkley, tucked away beneath Hawkley Hanger. Resisting the temptations to be found at the Hawkley Inn, you descend into the lush meadows of the Oakshott Valley, before a steep ascent on an old droving track to the top of Shoulder of Mutton Hill. Here, in a tranquil glade on its higher slopes, you will find a sarsen stone dedicated to Edward Thomas. With such surprising views across Steep and of 'sixty miles of South Downs at one glance', as Thomas described it, it is no wonder that he loved this area.

The return walk joins the Hangers Way, a 21-mile (33.8km) long distance trail traversing East Hampshire from Queen Elizabeth Country Park to Alton. Following a steep descent through a meadow, carpeted with cowslips in spring, as you follow the Oakshott Stream back to Hawkley.

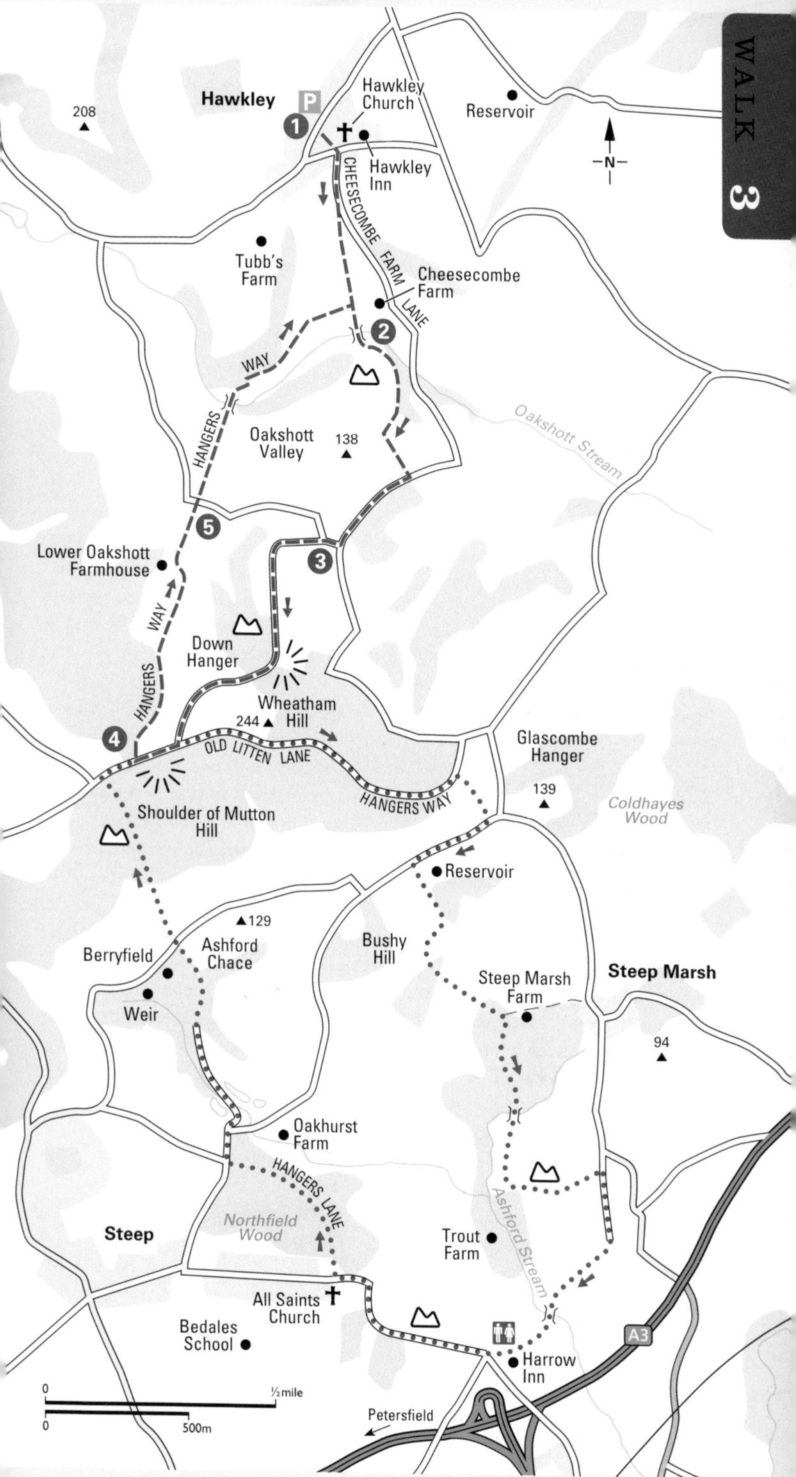

Hawkley
208
Hawkley Church
Reservoir
Hawkley Inn
N
CHEESECOMBE FARM LANE
Tubb's Farm
Cheesecombe Farm
WAY
HANGERS
Oaksholt Stream
Oakshott Valley
138
Lower Oakshott Farmhouse
WAY
HANGERS
Down Hanger
Wheatham Hill
244
OLD LITTEN LANE
Glascombe Hanger
HANGERS WAY
139
Coldhayes Wood
Shoulder of Mutton Hill
Reservoir
129
Bushy Hill
Berryfield
Ashford Chace
Steep Marsh Farm
Steep Marsh
Weir
94
Oakhurst Farm
HANGERS LANE
Ashford Stream
Northfield Wood
Steep
Trout Farm
All Saints Church
Bedales School
A3
Harrow Inn
0
½mile
0
500m
Petersfield

## WALK 3 DIRECTIONS

1 With your back to Hawkley church, walk left beside the green to the road junction. With the Hawkley Inn away to your left, cross over down Cheesecombe Farm Lane, signed 'Hangers Way'. Shortly, bear right along a concrete path. Descend past a broken stile and keep straight on at the fork of paths, with Cheesecombe Farm to the left.

### WHILE YOU'RE THERE

Track down the White Horse, at grid reference SU 714289, just off on the unclassified road from Petersfield to the A32. Known locally as 'the pub with no name', it's a classic example of an unspoilt country pub and was a regular haunt of Edward Thomas – his tankard still hangs in the bar. The pub inspired his first poem *Up in the Wind* (1914) and describes the inn's isolation. It begins with, 'I could wring the old thing's neck that put it there! A public-house'.

2 Cross Oakshott Stream and keep left along the field-edge beside woodland. Steeply ascend to a stile, keep right to a further stile, then turn left beside the fence and drop down to a track. Turn right, to reach a lane, then right again for 55yds (50m) to take the waymarked right of way beside Wheatham Hill House.

3 Climb the long and steep, chalky track up through Down Hanger (this gets very wet and muddy), with views east along the South Downs unfolding. At the top of Wheatham Hill, turn right at a T-junction of tracks along Old Litten Lane. In 300yds (274m), take the Hangers Way right over a stile. For the Edward Thomas memorial stone and magnificent

### WHERE TO EAT AND DRINK

Time your walk to coincide with lunch at the delightfully unspoilt, 16th-century Harrow Inn at Steep (credit cards not accepted). There are two characterful rooms with scrubbed wooden tables and warming winter fires. Expect ale straight from the cask, hearty soup and sandwiches, and a cottage garden for summer imbibing. The equally rustic Hawkley Inn offers a warm welcome to walkers, micro-brewery ales and imaginative home-cooked food.

South Downs views, continue along the track for 200yds (183m) and turn left with a waymarker. Pass beside the wooden barrier and drop down to the clearing on Shoulder of Mutton Hill.

4 Follow the Hangers Way as it descends through the edge of beech woods and steeply down across meadowland, eventually joining the drive to Lower Oakshott Farmhouse and a road.

5 Turn right, then left over the stile and follow the defined Hangers Way path through the Oakshott Valley, crossing stiles, plank bridges and delightful meadows to reach the junction of paths before Cheesecombe Farm. Turn left to the stile and retrace your steps all the way back to Hawkley and your car.

### WHAT TO LOOK OUT FOR

Two memorials in All Saints Church at Steep are worth looking for. One is to Basil Marden who was killed in an avalanche in the Andes in 1928; the other is to a Martha Legg who died in 1829 at the remarkable age of 105.

# Steep and the Hangers

*A longer walk takes in more of the distinctive scenery of the Hanger country.*

**See map and information panel for Walk 3**



**DISTANCE** *7.25 miles (11.7km)* **MINIMUM TIME** *4hrs*

**ASCENT/GRADIENT** *1,391ft (424m)* ▲▲▲ **LEVEL OF DIFFICULTY** +++

## WALK 4 DIRECTIONS (Walk 3 option)

Steep by name and steep by nature, the scattered village nestles on the lower slopes of the hangers that tower above the village and can be viewed as you descend Wheatham Hill. The village hides two more reminders of Thomas's time in the area.

On top of Wheatham Hill, follow the rutted track left for 0.5 mile (800m) downhill through the Ashford Hangers. Just before a lane, climb the stile right and descend through an avenue of trees and across a field to a stile and lane. Turn right then, in 400yds (366m), take the footpath left. Descend to a stile and bear gently right across the field to a stile by woodland. Turn left and follow the field-edge to Steep Marsh Farm. Turn right beside sheds and join a wooded track. Shortly, cross the drive and lawn to a house back into woodland. Cross a stream and, just before reaching a metalled drive, climb the steep path left beside trees to a stile. Follow the signed path across the field ahead to a stile, and continue to a lane. Turn right then, at a sharp left bend, bear off right into woodland. Walk above a small ravine and past timbered cottages to a footbridge. Continue ahead and pass the Harrow Inn. Turn right at the junction and walk uphill into Steep to All Saints Church.

The partly-Norman church lies close to Bedales School, which first attracted Thomas to the village in 1906, so that his children could attend the school. There's a memorial window to the poet by Lawrence Whistler (1912–2000) in the church.

Follow the Hangers Way opposite, across a playing field and down through Northfield Wood to a stile. Walk along the left-hand field-edge to a kissing gate and road. Turn right then, as it swings right, keep ahead up the footpath (the waterfall is to your left). At a junction, turn left and walk through light woodland to join a drive leading to a lane beside Ashford Chace.

Thomas lived in three houses in the village. You will find Berryfield, the poet's first home, next to Ashford Chace.

Turn right, then almost immediately left along a footpath towards Shoulder of Mutton Hill. Keep right at a fork to climb steeply up the grassy scarp slope to the memorial stone. At the top, keep ahead to reach a track. Turn right, then in 200yds (183m) turn left to join Walk 3 at Point 4.

WALK 5

# Emsworth – Harbour Delights

*Explore changing tides and fortunes on this breezy walk along Chichester Harbour's foreshore between Emsworth and Langstone.*

**DISTANCE** *4.5 miles (7.2km)* **MINIMUM TIME** *2hrs*

**ASCENT/GRADIENT** *Negligible* ▲▲▲ **LEVEL OF DIFFICULTY** +++

**PATHS** *Field-edge path, gravel or metalled shoreline paths, and short stretch along pebble foreshore*

**LANDSCAPE** *Foreshore and marshy coastline*

**SUGGESTED MAP** *OS Explorer 120 Chichester*

**START / FINISH** *Grid reference: SU 749056*

**DOG FRIENDLINESS** *Keep under control at all times*

**PARKING** *Pay-and-display car park in South Street, Emsworth*

**PUBLIC TOILETS** *Emsworth*

## WALK 5 DIRECTIONS

Situated at the head of one of the tidal creeks of Chichester Harbour, Emsworth is delightful with its attractive jumble of streets, lanes and alleys and yacht-filled harbour, is essentially a seafaring town. During the 18th and 19th centuries it was a principal port along this stretch of coast and became very prosperous through corn milling, boat building, fishing and a flourishing oyster industry.

The village still boasts shipwrights and chandleries, and fishing boats still work out of the harbour, but today it is more important as a yachting centre. If you stroll through the streets and by the harbour you can see the old tide mills that milled the grain from local farms, and see the houses built by wealthy merchants.

It's best to time this walk for low water – check the tides at www.easytide.ukho.gov.uk before leaving home. Turn right out of the car park and walk down South Street to the Quay. At the Quay, keep ahead to join the tarmac path that follows the causeway round the Mill Pond, adjacent to the main harbour.

Savour the views across the harbour, which are best at low tide, especially during the winter months when the mudflats are a haven to thousands of waders and wildfowl, including curlew, redshank, dunlin, shelduck and mallard. Take your binoculars with you on this walk, as birdlife abounds along its length. In winter, at high tide, you may see diving ducks like goldeneye and

### WHILE YOU'RE THERE

Stroll through the narrow streets, lined with specialist shops, then walk along the busy harbourside and around the two tidal mill ponds to capture the history and charm of this picturesque village. Emsworth Museum in North Street traces the history of the village.

**WHAT TO LOOK OUT FOR**

Look for the blue plaque on a house in Record Road. The author of the Jeeves and Wooster novels, P G Wodehouse, lived here between 1904 and 1913 and based many of his locations and characters on local places and people. Note the flint grave-watchers' huts in Warblington churchyard, built over 200 years ago, at a time when bodies were scarce for medical students to learn on.

red-breasted merganser in the harbour, while in the fields you are likely to spot brent geese feeding.

Pass beside Emsworth Sailing Club to join a concrete path above the shoreline. The path becomes gravelled as you near a grassy area at the entrance to Nore Barn Wood. Ignore the foreshore path here (impassable at high tides) and keep ahead through the edge of the wood to a gate. Beyond another gate, keep to the field-edge towards the ruined tower of Warblington Castle. Pass through more gates and shortly bear right into Warblington churchyard.

All that remains of Warblington Castle (private), an imposing fortified manor house built by the Countess of Salisbury between 1513 and 1526, is a tall brick turret visible through the trees. She was executed at the Tower of London in 1541 under the orders of Henry VIII due to her disapproval of his marriage to her friend Catherine of Aragon. The isolated church dates from the 13th century, a time when Warblington was the mother parish for Emsworth, and is well worth closer inspection. The churchyard is full of interesting gravestones, several with fine carvings reflecting tragedies at sea.

Turn left on exiting the main gate and turn right into the cemetery. Follow the metalled path round to the left and soon bear right to a gate into pasture. Bear diagonally left to a kissing gate on the harbour shore, and turn right along the sea wall path. Your path soon drops down on to the foreshore (access may be difficult at exceptionally high tides). In 200yds (183m) join a metalled path leading past Langstone's mills to reach the Royal Oak.

From its position at an important crossing point to Hayling Island and the availability of fresh water from the Lymbourne stream, Langstone grew into a thriving harbour village. You arrive at its seaward end, a delightful spot favoured by artists, complete with a pub, an old tide mill, windmill, and the broad expanse of Langstone Harbour with its tidal creeks, salt-marsh islands and mudflats. Much of this fragile landscape is now protected by a nature reserve.

Relax on one of the benches on the sea front and absorb the view across the harbour to Hayling Island before retracing your steps back to Emsworth.

**WHERE TO EAT AND DRINK**

There's a good choice of pubs, restaurants and tea rooms in Emsworth, notably the Greenhouse Café in the Square for home-made lunches and teas, Flintstones Tea Room on the Quay, and the Blue Bell and Coal Exchange pubs in South Street. The Royal Oak at Langstone is open all day and enjoys great harbour views.

WALK 6

# Jane Austen's Chawton

*A gentle ramble through the pastoral countryside that surrounds Chawton, where Jane Austen sought inspiration for her great novels.*

**DISTANCE** *5 miles (8km)* **MINIMUM TIME** *2hrs 30min*

**ASCENT/GRADIENT** *134ft (41m)* ▲▲▲ **LEVEL OF DIFFICULTY** +++

**PATHS** *Field paths, old railway track, some road walking, 12 stiles*

**LANDSCAPE** *Gently rolling farmland interspersed with woodland*

**SUGGESTED MAP** *OS Explorer 133 Haslemere & Petersfield*

**START / FINISH** *Grid reference: SU 708375* **DOG FRIENDLINESS** *Some stiles with gaps only suitable for small dogs; keep under control at all times*

**PARKING** *Free village car park opposite Jane Austen's House*

**PUBLIC TOILETS** *None; walkers may use toilets at Jane Austen's House*

Devoted followers of Jane Austen know and revere the village of Chawton, a quiet backwater off the A31 south of Alton, for it was here that she spent the last eight years of her life and where she wrote her major works. Since the successful dramatisation of her novels, interest in her personal life has increased dramatically and the village, or more significantly her home, has become internationally famous.

### Jane Austen's House

Jane Austen was born in Steventon, near Basingstoke, and spent the first 25 years of her life there before the family moved to Bath in 1801. Following spells in Clifton and Southampton, she moved to Chawton Cottage with her mother and sister Cassandra in July 1809. Her house, now simply called Jane Austen's House, belonged to her brother Edward who had inherited the estate of Chawton from his uncle Thomas Knight, whose family had purchased the manor in 1578. It was Edward who renovated the building, adding three further bedrooms, so that his mother and sisters could live in comfort and entertain friends. Jane wrote about the cottage to her brother Francis Austen in 1809:

*'Our Chawton House, how much we find*
*Already in it to our mind:*
*And convinced, that when complete*
*It will all other houses beat*
*That ever have been made or mended*
*With rooms concise and rooms distended'*

It was at Chawton Cottage that she spent her most active writing phase. At a small table in the living room she began to revise her earlier manuscript novels – *Sense and Sensibility*, *Pride and Prejudice* and *Northanger Abbey* – and then wrote her great novels *Mansfield Park*, *Emma* and *Persuasion*. Jane became ill in 1816 and moved to Winchester to seek medical advice. She died in 1817 aged 41 and is buried in Winchester Cathedral.

You can visit the charming red-brick house which has been beautifully restored to look as it would have done in the 1800s. It is more than a museum, as it succeeds in capturing the atmosphere of her modest lifestyle through collections of family mementoes and documentary material which give a real insight into her life and writings. View the drawing room, the parlour where she wrote her novels, and the bedrooms, then browse in the bookshop and enjoy a picnic in the flower-filled garden.

## Tea at Farringdon

Our walk explores some of the peaceful open countryside through which Jane Austen would have strolled. The furthest point on the walk is Upper Farringdon. She often visited the village to see Harriet Benn whose father was the vicar of All Saints Church. 'Harriet Benn' she wrote, 'sleeps at the Great House (Chawton House) to-night and spends to-morrow with us; and the plan is that we should all walk with her to drink tea at Faringdon'.

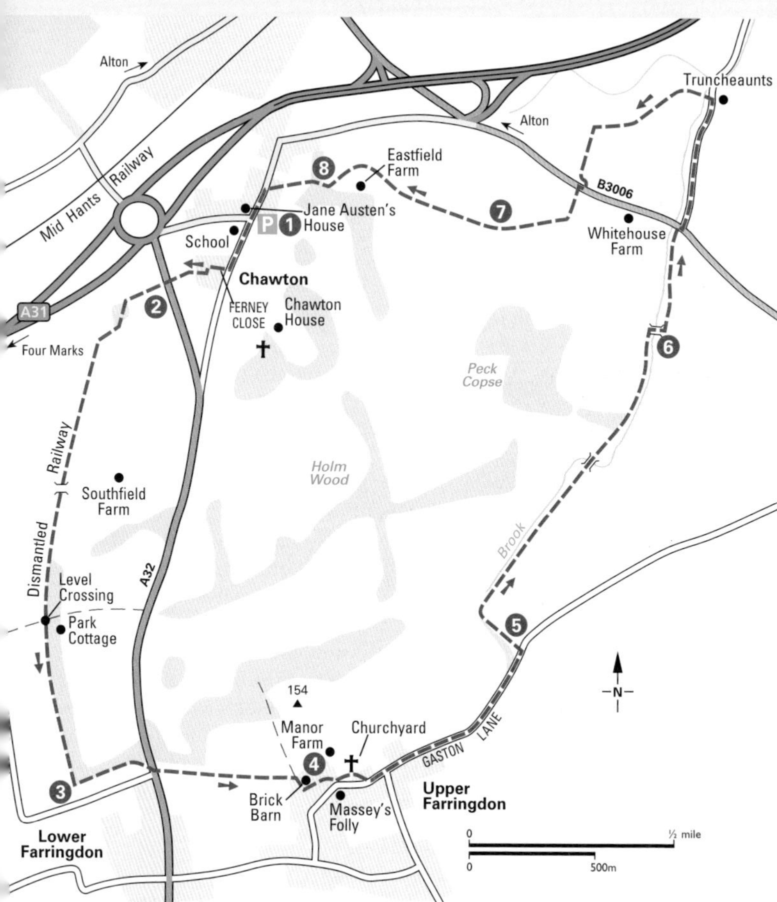


## WALK 6 DIRECTIONS

**1** Turn left out of the car park, opposite Jane Austen's House, and walk along a dead-end lane. Pass the school and turn right into Ferney Close. Keep to the left and bear left along a path beside

Ferney Bungalow to a stile. Cross and continue along the enclosed path to a stile and cross (with care) the A32.

❷ Climb steps, go through a kissing-gate and walk along the field edge, leading to a gap on your left. Go through a copse, following the path right, then left, between fields. Keep straight ahead along a former railway track, go under a brick arch bridge, and continue for 650yds (594m) beyond the barn and level crossing near Park Cottage.

❸ Just before a second arch, swing left off the old railway and follow the field-edge track past metal silos to a stile. Cross the A32 and join a track leading to Manor Farm. At a crossing of tracks, before a brick barn, turn right. In a few paces, take the narrow fenced path left to reach a track.

**WHAT TO LOOK OUT FOR**

Massey's Folly, an enormous red-brick building, in Upper Farringdon is probably the strangest building in Hampshire. With 17 bedrooms and two towers, its purpose is unknown but since 1925 has been used as a school and village hall.

❹ Turn right to the lane in Upper Farringdon, opposite Massey's Folly. Turn left into the churchyard and leave by the main gate, turning left along the lane. Keep ahead along Gaston Lane for 0.5 mile (800m) to a track on your left.

❺ Turn left; then, shortly, take the grassy track right. Climb the stile ahead into open pasture, following the brook on your left to a second stile; after 170yds

**WHERE TO EAT AND DRINK**

Opposite Jane Austen's House you'll find Cassandra's Cup, renowned for home-baked cakes, cream teas and hot savoury snacks at lunchtime (seasonal opening). Along the lane is the Greyfriar (open all day) with a sheltered garden and offering daily specials.

(155m) cross the bridge over the brook on your left. Keep going, with the brook to your right, to a stile at the end of the field.

❻ Cross the brook, and follow it to the B3006. Bear right, then cross the road to join a tarmac track and follow it to Truncheaunts Farm. Cross the stile at the fingerpost, then the footbridge and follow the right-hand field edge. Drop down steps by a silo, bear left past the metal barn and follow the track to the B3006, opposite Shepherds Court. Cross over, turn right along the verge and turn left through a gate. Walk down a concrete track and turn right through a gate at the end. Follow the right-hand field-edge to a gate.

❼ Bear right across the field to reach stiles set in the hedge and maintain your direction across three more fields and stiles towards Eastfield Farm. Skirt round the farm via yellow-topped squeeze stiles and kissing gates through several fields to reach a gate beside woodland, which is located beyond a corrugated iron shed.

❽ Go though the copse to a stile and then bear half left across the field to a gate. Continue ahead to a gate in the wall and walk along a narrow footpath back to the main village street. Turn left back to the car park.

# In the Footsteps of Gilbert White at Selborne

*A walk through the glorious beech hangers and tranquil meadows that so inspired the eminent naturalist Gilbert White.*



**DISTANCE** *3.5 miles (5.6km)* **MINIMUM TIME** *2hrs*

**ASCENT/GRADIENT** *361ft (110m)* ▲▲▲ **LEVEL OF DIFFICULTY** +++

**PATHS** *Woodland, field paths, stretch of metalled road, 6 stiles*

**LANDSCAPE** *Lofty beech hangers, lush rolling pasture and woodland*

**SUGGESTED MAP** *OS Explorer 133 Haslemere & Petersfield*

**START / FINISH** *Grid reference: SU 742334*

**DOG FRIENDLINESS** *Dogs should be kept under control at all times*

**PARKING** *Free National Trust car park behind Selborne Arms*

**PUBLIC TOILETS** *At car park in Selborne*

Selborne, and its beautiful surrounding countryside, were made famous over two centuries ago by the writings and reputation of the clergyman and pioneer naturalist Gilbert White who published *The Natural History and Antiquities of Selborne* in 1789. Based on 40 years of observation and meticulous recording of the flora and fauna around the village, it is one of the few books on natural history to gain the rank of an English classic. White poetically describes his day-to-day experiences of nature in the Hampshire countryside through a series of letters to his friends Thomas Pennant and Daines Barrington.

## Local Boy

Born in the village in 1720, White was the grandson of a vicar of Selborne, and, having been ordained after attending Oxford, he returned to live in the village to serve as a curate at neighbouring parishes and at Selborne in 1751. From the age of ten until his death in 1793 he lived at The Wakes, a large rambling house that overlooks the village green (the Plestor) and church. Although the village has changed, White would find the surrounding landscape that he knew and loved so well largely unspoilt and now preserved by the National Trust.

This walk literally follows in White's footsteps, exploring the lofty, beech-clad hills or 'hangers' that rise steeply behind his home, and the lush 'lythes' or meadows beyond St Mary's Church, both beautiful areas through which he would stroll and passionately observe and note the wildlife around him. The walk comprises two loops around the village, so if you are short of time (or energy) you can enjoy the classic climb on to Selborne Common and still have time to visit Gilbert White's home, now a museum.

## Up the Zig-Zag Path

The walk begins with a long ascent to the top of Selborne Hill and Common, a task made easier by the hard work put in by Gilbert White and his brother John in 1753, when they constructed the famous Zig-Zag path up the steep scarp face. White described the Common as 'a vast hill of chalk, rising three hundred feet above the village; and is divided into a sheep down, the high wood, and a long hanging wood called The Hanger'. You are rewarded with peace and tranquillity when you reach White's Wishing Stone, and magnificent views over the village. You can explore the maze of paths that criss-cross the Common, but the main route threads through the glorious beech hangers to White's favourite viewpoint. Here White would pause to absorb the breathtaking cameo that took in his home, the church and the serene wooded landscape.

Back in the village, locate White's grave in the churchyard and visit St Mary's Church. Here you will find White's fine memorial window depicting St Francis of Assisi preaching to 82 birds, all of which are mentioned in his book. The second loop heads east through the Oakhanger Valley, following the Hangers Way to Priory Farm, the site of Selborne Priory.

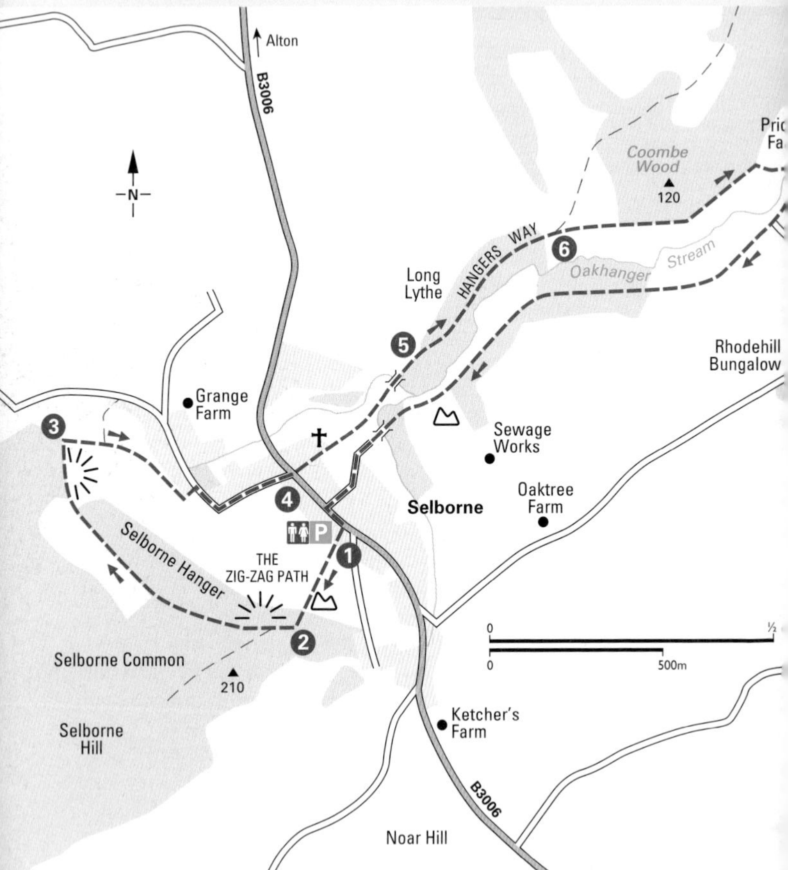


## WALK 7 DIRECTIONS

❶ Take the arrowed footpath, signed 'The zig-zag and Hanger', by the car park entrance and gently ascend to a gate at the base of Selborne Common. Bear left to follow the impressive Zig-Zag path uphill, pausing at regular intervals to admire the unfolding view across the village.

❷ At the top, take the stepped path right and, in a few paces,



*Right: Selborne (Walk 7).*

keep right at a fork to follow the lower path through the beech hangers. Shortly, look out for a metal bench, by a path ascending from the right, and savour the splendid view of the church and The Wakes through the gap in the trees. Continue along the main path, gently descending to a junction of paths, by a National Trust sign.

**3** Turn right downhill along a track then, where this curves left, bear off right across a stile into pasture. Keep to the left-hand edge, cross two more stiles and follow the enclosed path to a lane. Turn right and follow it back into the village, opposite the church. Turn right along the B3006 road for The Wakes and the car park, if you wish to cut the walk short.

**WHERE TO EAT AND DRINK**

Delicious light lunches, cakes and afternoon teas can be enjoyed in the civilised Tea Parlour at The Wakes, Gilbert White's house. Alternatively, try one of the two pubs, The Selborne Arms, which has a family room, or the Queens Inn for home-cooked bar food.

**4** Cross the B road and follow the Hangers Way sign through the churchyard to a gate. Follow the defined path to a footbridge over the Oakhanger Stream.

**5** Keep to the Hangers Way through a gate and along the edge of meadowland to a gate, then pass through a stretch of woodland to a kissing gate and fork of paths.

**6** Proceed straight ahead (yellow arrow), leaving the Hangers Way. Eventually pass alongside a fence to a stile on the edge of Coombe Wood. Keep close to the woodland fringe to a stile,

**WHAT TO LOOK FOR**

Note the trunk of a great yew tree in the churchyard which is estimated to be 1,400 years old. By the time it blew down in 1990 its girth measured 26ft (8m) and was taller than the church. Opposite The Wakes is the old butchers shop. It is hidden by two of the four original lime trees, planted by Gilbert White in 1756, to hide 'the blood and filth' from view as he worked in his parlour. Look for the splendid Victorian iron drinking fountain at the south end of the village. It is in the form of a fierce lion's head flanked by windmills.

then bear left along the field-edge to a stile and turn right along a bridleway towards Priory Farm. Keep to the track through the farmyard to the metalled drive.

**7** In a few paces, where the drive curves left, bear off right along a track beside a bungalow. Go through a gate and follow the grassy track uphill along the field-edge, through a gate, eventually reaching a gate and woodland. Follow the track (can be muddy) through beech woodland. Leave the wood, passing a house called Dorton's, and climb the lane steeply back to Selborne, turning left for the car park.

**WHILE YOU'RE THERE**

Visit Gilbert White's house. Learn more about the famous naturalist and visit exhibitions commemorating the naturalist and explorer Francis Oates, who journeyed to South America and South Africa, and Captain Lawrence Oates who accompanied Scott on his ill-fated expedition to the South Pole in 1911.

# Odiham and the Basingstoke Canal

*Combining elegant Odiham with a castle and the leafy Basingtoke Canal.*



**DISTANCE** *4.5 miles (7.2km)* **MINIMUM TIME** *2hrs*
**ASCENT/GRADIENT** *147ft (45m)* ▲▲▲ **LEVEL OF DIFFICULTY** +++
**PATHS** *Canal tow path, field-edge and woodland, 4 stiles*
**LANDSCAPE** *Farmland, parkland, woodland and residential area*
**SUGGESTED MAP** *OS Explorer 144 Basingstoke, Alton & Whitchurch*
**START / FINISH** *Grid reference: SU 740510*
**DOG FRIENDLINESS** *Scoop poop on the tow path; keep under control in fields*
**PARKING** *Odiham High Street or signed pay-and-display car parks*
**PUBLIC TOILETS** *None en route*

Flanked by the expanding towns of Aldershot and Basingstoke, and the M3, Odiham retains an unspoilt, country-town atmosphere and is one of Hampshire's most elegant small towns. Handsome Georgian houses and colour-washed, timber-framed cottages line the wide main street, including the George Hotel, first licensed in 1540, and Kingston House, built in the 18th century of local brick in Flemish bond. Some highlights include the 14th-century church, The Bury with its stocks and whipping-post, and the Tudor vicarage.

## Canal Link to London

Inextricably linked with the town is the Basingstoke Canal. When it opened in 1794, Odiham Wharf saw shipments of timber, grain, malt, coal and various manufactured goods. This once popular commercial route, linking London with North Hampshire, climbed through Surrey via 29 locks. The waterway also had 69 bridges, two aqueducts, active wharfs and warehouses and, at 37 miles (59.5km), was the longest canal in southern England. The coming of the railways led to its gradual decline, although it was used to transport materials for the construction of Aldershot Garrison in the 1850s and for shifting munitions during the First World War. During the Second World War the canal formed a useful lowland link in a line of defence created between Margate and Bristol. Following a period of restoration, 32 miles (51.5km) of the canal re-opened as a leisure amenity in 1991.

Many regard the canal as a linear country park. The clean spring water supply harbours a rich wildlife and forms one of Britain's finest areas for aquatic plants. Surprisingly though, the canal is more famous for bats. The disused 1,230yd (1,119m) Greywell Tunnel – home to some 12,500 bats of all native species, including Natterer's and Daubenton's bats – is the largest bat roost in Britain. Return to the tunnel entrance at dusk to watch the spectacle of thousands of bats leaving to feed. Set adjacent to the tow path you'll also see the picturesque ruins of King John's Castle, sometimes known as Odiham Castle. Built in 1212, it was used by King John as a resting place between Windsor and Winchester.

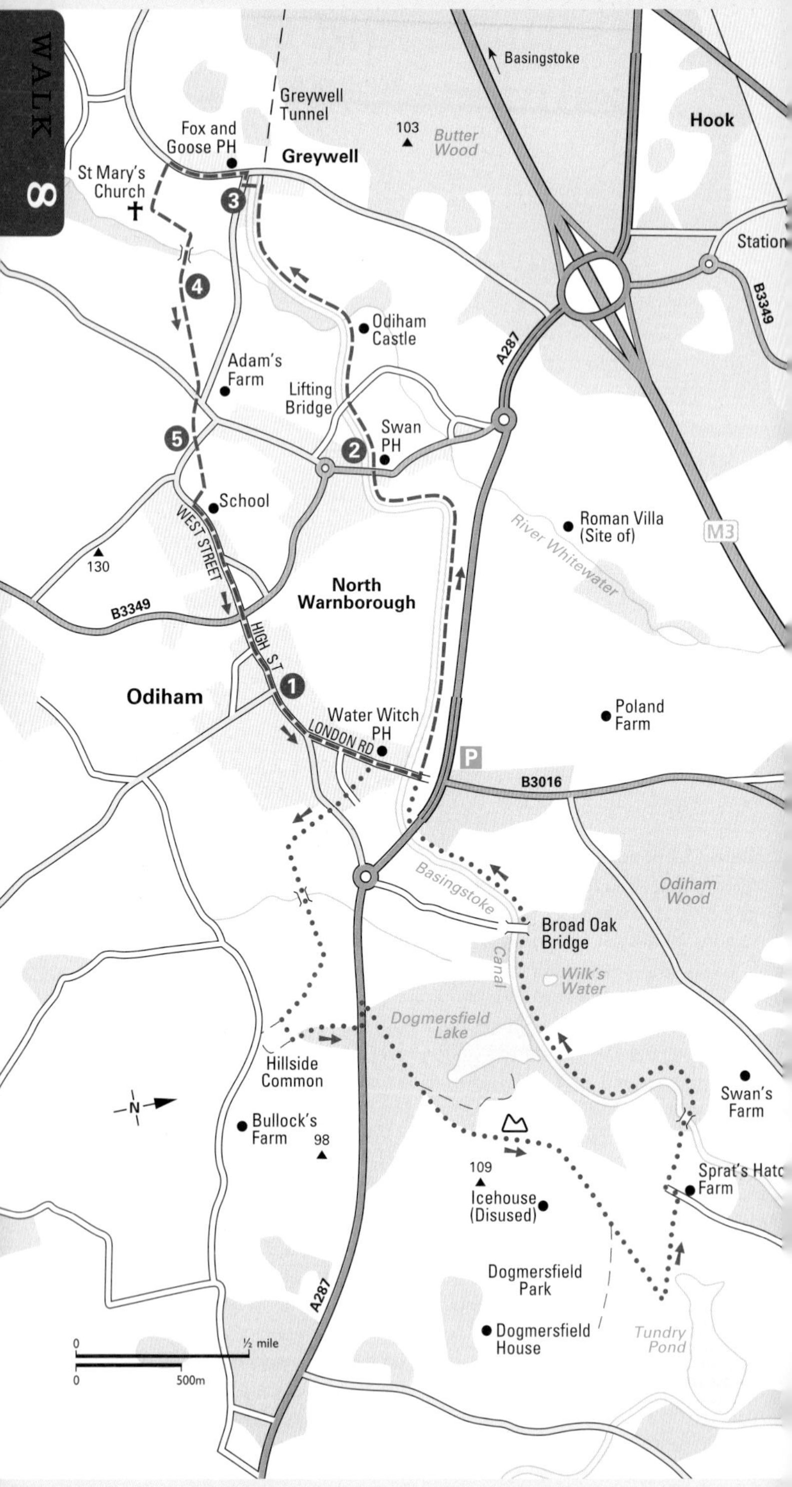
WALK 8
Basingstoke
Greywell Tunnel
103
Butter Wood
Hook
Fox and Goose PH
Greywell
St Mary's Church
3
Station
4
B3349
Odiham Castle
A287
Adam's Farm
Lifting Bridge
Swan PH
5
2
School
Roman Villa (Site of)
River Whitewater
M3
WEST STREET
130
North Warnborough
B3349
HIGH ST
Odiham
1
Poland Farm
Water Witch PH
LONDON RD
P
B3016
Basingstoke
Odiham Wood
Broad Oak Bridge
Canal
Wilk's Water
Dogmersfield Lake
Hillside Common
Swan's Farm
N
Bullock's Farm
98
109
Sprat's Hatc Farm
Icehouse (Disused)
Dogmersfield Park
A287
Tundry Pond
Dogmersfield House
0
½ mile
0
500m

## WALK 8 DIRECTIONS

1 Head east along the High Street and take the left fork, London Road, leading to the Basingstoke Canal. Pass the Water Witch pub and cross the bridge, then drop down left to the tow path. Follow the waterway parallel with the A287 for just over a mile (1.6km) to North Warnborough.

2 Pass the Swan pub and go under the adjacent road bridge. Keep to the tow path, passing a lifting bridge, then in 300yds (274m) pass the ruins of Odiham Castle (or King John's Castle) on your right. Pass over the River Whitewater and continue for 0.5 mile (800m) to Greywell Tunnel, famous for its roosting bat population and best visited at dusk. Take the path left over its portal and drop down to the road.

### WHAT TO LOOK OUT FOR

The tow path is a good place for birding. You may see mallards, wagtails, herons, little grebe, summer migrants like spotted flycatcher, willow warbler, and swallows skimming low over the water, and, if you're lucky, the blue flash of the kingfisher. Dragonflies and butterflies abound and you may spot a pike feeding in the shallows.

3 Turn right into Greywell, and then left at the junction to pass the Fox and Goose. Walk through the village and turn left through the lychgate to St Mary's Church. Walk down the path to the church and turn left through the gate opposite. Walk across the field for 180yds (165m) to a stile; now,turn right to a stile and bridge to cross over the River Whitewater and enter Greywell Moors Nature Reserve.

### WHERE TO EAT AND DRINK

You'll find several pubs in North Warnborough, the most convenient being the Swan beside the canal, and the Fox and Goose in Greywell. There are no refreshment stops on Walk 9, but Odiham has a good range of pubs, notably the George in the High Street, and a couple of tea rooms.

4 Walk through the reserve, passing a memorial to the eminent botanist E C Wallace, and bear left to walk in an easterly direction across the field to the road. Turn left for 50yds (46m), then right with the footpath sign. After a few paces dodge left through a gap in the hedge, then bear diagonally across a paddock and keep ahead across the next field to a road.

5 Cross to the stile opposite and walk across the field, heading to the right of three chimneys, to a stile. Join a path beside a school, turning right to reach West Street. Turn left, passing the school, then as the road veers left, bear right up West Street to the roundabout. Go straight over and back along Odiham High Street.

### WHILE YOU'RE THERE

Stroll around Odiham. Behind All Saints Church and near an almshouses built in 1625, is a pest house of about the same date. Constructed to isolate suspected sufferers of the plague until they recovered or died, this fine example is one of only a few that survive in Hampshire today. Converted to a private house in 1780, it is now a museum. In the churchyard are the graves of several French prisoners. They were held at a camp in an old chalk pit on the Alton road during the Napoleonic war and it is thought they helped build the Basingstoke Canal.

# Dogmersfield Park



*Combine this loop with Walk 8 to create a figure-of-eight.*

**See map and information panel for Walk 8**

**DISTANCE** *5.5 miles (8.8km)* **MINIMUM TIME** *2hrs 30min*

**ASCENT/GRADIENT** *147ft (45m)* ▲▲▲ **LEVEL OF DIFFICULTY** +++

## WALK 9 DIRECTIONS (Walk 8 option)

Head east along High Street and fork left into London Road. Turn right opposite a postbox, following a signed footpath along a drive and crossing several stiles to reach a road. Cross straight over, and follow the field-edge path to a junction at the third kissing gate. Turn left to a bridge over a stream then bear left over a stile and head diagonally across a field to a stile.

Keep ahead for 60yds (55m) to a stile by a cattle trough, cross it and turn right along the field-edge to a gap in the hedge. Bear right beside a fenced paddock then bear left across a drive to a kissing gate. Continue beside a fence to a second kissing gate, cross a plank bridge and turn left on to a woodland path to reach the A287.

Dogmersfied House was built in 1728 on the site of a medieval Bishop's Palace. Henry VII came here with his son Prince Arthur to meet the Spanish Catherine of Aragon. Following this visit, Arthur married Catherine but soon died, leaving his brother Henry VIII to inherit the throne.

Cross over the A287 then turn left, and soon turn right between the gatehouses into Dogmersfield Park. Follow the gravel track to a junction near Dogmersfield Lake, then fork right on to a green lane to a kissing gate beneath power lines. Keep ahead along a farm track and join a metalled estate road past a huddle of Tudor-style buildings to a cattle grid and footpath sign. Fork left along the fenced green track towards Tundry Pond.

Just beyond a newly planted copse, turn sharp left at the footpath sign on to an estate road. Fork right just before the ornamental gates, to walk along an enclosed path to a kissing gate at Sprat's Hatch Farm. Turn left on to the bridleway, bear right, then cross the canal and turn left on to the tow path.

Follow the short woodland path beside Wilk's Water to reach a fanciful brick house known as King John's Hunting Lodge. Built in the 18th century to ornament the superb view from Dogmersfield House, it is difficult to reason why the building is linked to King John, as his hunting lodges were stone and timber not brick structures.

Keep to the towpath for 1.5 miles (2.4km), passing under Broad Oak Bridge and the A287. Shortly, leave the tow path at the next bridge and follow London Road back into Odiham.

*Left: Whitewater River, near Odiham (Walks 8 & 9)*

# Portsmouth's Naval Heritage

*Step back in time around the streets, quays and dockyards of Old Portsmouth.*

**DISTANCE** *3 miles (4.8km)* **MINIMUM TIME** *2hrs 30min*

**ASCENT/GRADIENT** *Negligible* ▲▲▲ **LEVEL OF DIFFICULTY** +++

**PATHS** *Sea wall defences, cobbled streets and pavements*

**LANDSCAPE** *Historic streets, docklands, busy harbour and waterfront*

**SUGGESTED MAP** *OS Explorer 119 Meon Valley and AA town plan*

**START / FINISH** *Grid reference: SU 634990*

**DOG FRIENDLINESS** *Not suitable for dogs*

**PARKING** *Clarence Pier car park (right of Amusement Park)*

**PUBLIC TOILETS** *Broad Street, Gunwharf Quays and the Hard*

## WALK 10 DIRECTIONS

Portsmouth has been the home of the Royal Navy for more than 800 years, playing a key role in the defence of the British Empire and synonymous with Nelson's victory at Trafalgar. It was from here that many of Britain's great naval heroes set sail to earn their place in history and their legacy lives on in Old Portsmouth, with its quaint houses, colourful waterfront and historic dockyard. Walk along the fortifications, through the cobbled streets of Spice Island, once filled with sailors and press gangs, and discover Britain's naval heritage by touring the dockyard, museums and exhibitions.

From the car park, join the Millennium Promenade (Renaissance Trail) and cross the footbridge. Follow the chain-link trail (marked on the paving) along the sea wall away from Clarence Pier towards the ruined Garrison Church.

Founded in 1212 as a hospice for travellers and the sick, the Garrison Church was where Charles II married his Portuguese bride, Catherine of Braganza, in 1662. It was reduced to its roofless state by bombing during the Blitz in World War Two. Continue along the wall to the restored Square Tower and proceed to the Round Tower, both built during the 15th century to protect the dockyard. Follow the chain-link paving down the steps on to Tower Street and into West Street, passing weatherboarded Quebec House, the oldest house in Old Portsmouth (1754), to the Still and West pub and the Point, the heart of Spice Island.

This tiny peninsula of narrow cobbled lanes lay outside the

**WHERE TO EAT AND DRINK**

There's a wide choice of pubs and cafés, including the Spice Island Inn, the Still & West and Sally Port Tea Rooms in Old Portsmouth. There are waterfront bars and cafés at Gunwharf Quays and at many of the attractions on the route.

**WHAT TO LOOK FOR**

As you stroll down the High Street, look for George Court, formerly the George Hotel, and the inscription recording that Nelson stayed there before joining HMS Victory and setting off for the Battle of Trafalgar. The Duke of Buckingham was murdered in a nearby house in 1628; a plaque can be seen on the wall.

17th-century walls and during the 18th and 19th centuries was bursting with all the life, danger and excitement one associates with a thriving naval port. At one time, it was said, 2,000 prostitutes and 200 beer houses could be found here, along with gambling saloons and cock fighting.

Curve right, following the chain-link along Broad Street, then left along Feltham Row, passing between the old fishing harbour and new housing developments to White Hart Road. Turn left, pass the Fish Market and continue ahead along Gunwharf Road, passing the Isle of Wight Ferry Terminal. Follow the chain-link left towards the terminal building, then right into the Gunwharf Quays complex.

The waterfront land here, closed to the public for centuries, has now been opened up for everyone to enjoy. There are public promenades, viewing terraces for maritime events and berths for tall ships, and the bright and bustling Gunwharf Quays complex now features cafés, bars, restaurants, a 14-screen cinema and more than 90 shops.

Follow the trail around the lock, then turn right through Central Square. Pass under the railway and turn left to the Hard beyond Portsmouth Harbour Station. Turn left to the Naval Dockyard and Flagship Portsmouth.

Allow plenty of time to visit the site, for there is much to see and explore. See the spot where Nelson died on HMS *Victory*, view the hull of Henry VIII's favourite warship, which sank in 1545 with the loss of 700 men and dramatically rose again from the sea bed in 1982, then step back in time and experience life aboard a Tudor warship by visiting the amazing *Mary Rose* Exhibition. Explore the four vast decks of HMS *Warrior*, Britain's first iron-clad battleship, built in 1860, and discover more about the Navy in the absorbing Royal Navy Museum.

Return along the Hard, pass St George's Church, go under the railway and keep ahead along St George's Road with the sports field on your left. Bear left at the junction with Gunwharf Road

**WHILE YOU'RE THERE**

Enjoy a leisurely 50-minute cruise around Portsmouth Harbour and view the warships and fortifications like Portchester Castle. Visit 393 Old Commercial Road, the Georgian house where Charles Dickens was born in 1812. Furnished in early 19th-century style, it houses a museum containing many items associated with the novelist.

to the roundabout. Continue ahead to visit the City Museum; otherwise, at the roundabout, turn right along High Street to the cathedral. Turn left just past the Sally Port Inn into Grand Parade and join the path past Garrison Church and across Nelson's Bridge to return to the car park.

WALK 11

# William and the Silent Whistles

*A rural ramble around the Forest of Bere.*

**DISTANCE** *4.5 miles (7.2km)* **MINIMUM TIME** *2hrs*

**ASCENT/GRADIENT** *213ft (65m)* ▲▲▲ **LEVEL OF DIFFICULTY** +++

**PATHS** *Bridleways and forest tracks – will be muddy after rain*

**LANDSCAPE** *Old railway path, river valley and mature woodland*

**SUGGESTED MAP** *OS Explorer 119 Meon Valley & Portsmouth*

**START / FINISH** *Grid reference: SU 574116*

**DOG FRIENDLINESS** *Run free on the old railway and in West Walk*

**PARKING** *Station Car Park, Wickham*

**PUBLIC TOILETS** *Station Road, Wickham*

With its medieval market square and engaging collection of independent shops, Wickham is one of Hampshire's most attractive little towns. It was the birthplace of William of Wykeham, founder of both Winchester College and New College, Oxford.

Despite his humble peasant background William led a charmed life, and by the time he was appointed Bishop of Winchester in 1367 he was a wealthy man. He transformed the interior of his great Norman cathedral, and personally endowed the two prestigious colleges that still flourish more than six hundred years after his death. William had been educated in Winchester, where he caught the eye of Bishop Edington, who introduced him to Edward III.

In a secular career spanning twenty years, William rose to be Chief Surveyor of the Royal Castles and Warden of Forests and Woods. It was a fitting appointment, for in those days Wickham lay at the heart of the Forest of Bere, a vast woodland stretching from the Sussex border to the River Test. Saxon kings hunted here since long before the Norman Conquest, but in 1086 King William formally declared Bere as a Royal hunting forest. When Charles I led the last Royal hunt in 1628, most of the trees had been felled to provide timber for the naval dockyards along the south coast.

Nevertheless, timber remains an important industry and a large timber yard still flourishes beside the former railway goods yard at Mislingford. The Meon Valley railway arrived late on the Hampshire landscape, a product of territorial skirmishing between the London & South Western Railway and its arch-rival, the Great Western. In an effort to protect its south coast traffic from the Great Western railheads at Basingstoke and Winchester, the L&SWR opened its own route from Alton to Fareham in 1903.

Built to main line standards with gentle curves and easy gradients, the new line was an expensive white elephant. From the start it generated little revenue, drifting through the inter-war years towards the inevitable closure in 1955. Yet the Meon Valley railway has its place in history. Early in June 1944, Sir Winston Churchill and his War Cabinet met other Allied leaders in a special train at Droxford Station to complete their plans for the D-Day invasion of Europe.

With steam whistles now a distant memory, much of the old line has a new role as a peaceful bridleway. This walk follows it up the valley before plunging into West Walk, a charming mixture of 19th-century oak and modern conifer plantations that forms the largest surviving fragment of the former Royal forest. The area is now a Forest Nature Reserve, with a variety of visitor facilities.



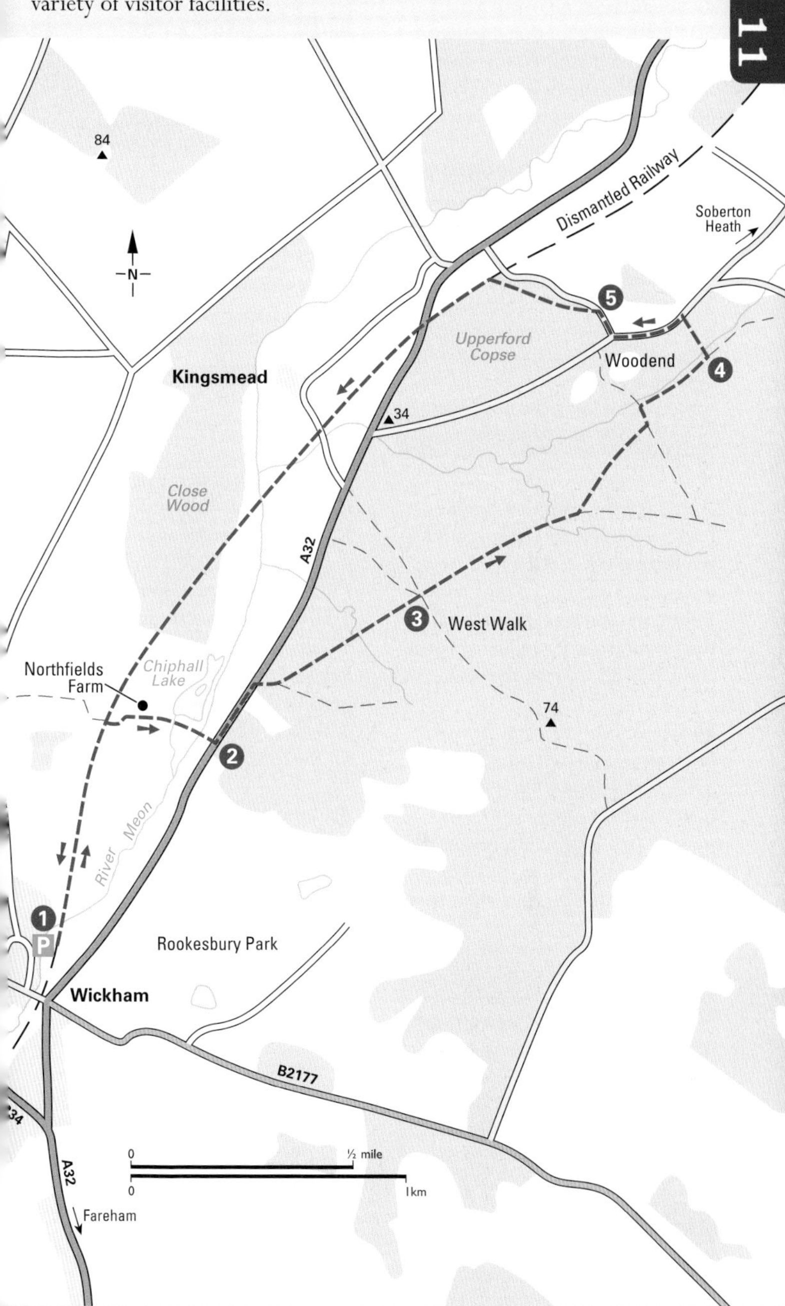

## WALK 11 DIRECTIONS

1 The Station car park on the north-east outskirts of Wickham backs directly on to the bridleway. Turn left, heading north and leaving the bridge over the River Meon behind you. Follow the old line as far as the first overbridge; 60yds (55m) beyond the brick arch, take the path that doubles back to the left and climb up to the farm track at the top. Turn left, cross over the railway and follow the track as it winds past the picturesque Northfields Farm and Chiphall Lake to the A32.

### WHAT TO LOOK OUT FOR

The lavish scale of the bridges and earthworks along the old railway path tell their own tale of thwarted ambition. Although the line was built wide enough for double track, it opened with just a single line – and traffic was so disappointing that the second track was never laid.

2 There is no footway here so cross over, turn left, and take great care as you follow the busy main road for 200yds (183m), passing two lodge cottages on the right-hand side. Then, just beyond Chiphall Paddock, turn right past a wooden barrier into West Walk. Follow the gravelled track at right angles to the road for the first 75yds (69m), then fork left on to a forest path. Ignore all turnings, and keep ahead as the trail dips into a small valley, crosses a brook, and climbs 300yds (274m) to a five-way junction.

### WHILE YOU'RE THERE

Children will love exploring the secret tunnels and underground chambers at the fully restored Fort Nelson. One of a chain of Victorian forts on Portsdown Hill, it was built to defend Portsmouth from the threat of a Napoleonic invasion that never came. The fort is open daily throughout the year (except Christmas) with guided tours, family events and the fully licensed Powderkeg Café.

### WHERE TO EAT AND DRINK

Wickham has a good choice of pubs, restaurants and tea rooms, including the King's Head for Fuller's ales and home-cooked specials, and the 15th-century Wickham Wine Bar and Restaurant. Light lunches and afternoon teas are served at Lilly's tea and coffee house.

3 Keep ahead here, signed towards West Walk and Woodend. Continue over the next crossways (signed 'West Walk') and, 220yds (201m) further on, fork left onto a narrower gravel track. Keep ahead at a crossways, then fork left, dropping down to cross a gravelled forest ride. Continue for 320yds (293m), and take a turning on the left.

4 Immediately cross a tiny brook, climb the short hill and, after 200yds (183m), leave the forest at a gate on the road to Soberton Heath. Turn left, then take the first turning on the right, signposted to Swanmore and Curdridge. Follow the road for 250yds (229m), as far as a small lay-by on the left-hand side.

5 Here you'll find the start of a rather unpromising little path, which improves as it drops down beside a post and rail fence towards the old railway. Join the old line just south of the road bridge and turn left, for 2 miles (3.2km), back to the start.

# The Cradle of Cricket



*Across to Broadhalfpenny Down, historic home to Hambledon Cricket Club.*

**DISTANCE** *6 miles (9.7km)* **MINIMUM TIME** *2hrs 45min*

**ASCENT/GRADIENT** *420ft (128m)* ▲▲▲ **LEVEL OF DIFFICULTY** +++

**PATHS** *Field paths, farm tracks and stretches of road, 16 stiles*

**LANDSCAPE** *Rolling farmland and chalk downland*

**SUGGESTED MAP** *OS Explorer 119 Meon Valley*

**START / FINISH** *Grid reference: SU 646150*

**DOG FRIENDLINESS** *Keep dogs under control at all times*

**PARKING** *Street parking near Hambledon village centre*

**PUBLIC TOILETS** *None en route*

Hambledon is steeped in cricketing history. Broadhalfpenny Down, 2 miles (3.2km) north-east of the village, has echoed with the sound of leather on willow since 1750, a time when the game was played with a curved bat and two forked sticks as stumps. Although cricket had been played in other parts of England, it was Hambledon Cricket Club that formulated the rules of the modern game and promoted the growth of club cricket.

## Successful Club

Hambledon became known as 'the cradle of cricket' through the successes of the club between 1772 and 1781. They won 23 of 39 matches played against All England teams, and became famous throughout the world. Their greatest victory was in 1777 when they won by an innings and 168 runs in a match played for 1,000 guineas. Matches became memorable affairs, with thousands of spectators travelling miles to witness sporting history. The Bat and Ball public house was built in 1730 and served as a pavilion and clubhouse. Instrumental in the success of the club was landlord Richard Nyren, a great all-rounder, who became club captain, secretary, groundsman and an authority on the rules of the game.

When Nyren moved to the George Hotel in the village, the club left Broadhalfpenny Down and continued with equal success on Windmill Down. The gradual decline of Hambledon Cricket Club coincided with the formation of Marylebone Cricket Club in 1787 and the administration of the game moving from Hambledon to Lord's, the London cricket ground established by Thomas Lord, who was president of the Hambledon club at the time. When Nyren left Hambledon in 1791 the club broke up and nothing further is known about the club until about 1857, when a ground was established at Ridge Meadow near Park Farm.

Walk here on a summer weekend and you are bound to find a match in progress, either at Ridge Meadow or Broadhalfpenny Down. Relax with a drink outside the Bat and Ball, view the classic English scene and muse over the glory days when Richard Nyren led the village team out to face the mighty England players in front of huge crowds. Across the road from the inn you'll find the memorial stone, inscribed with two bats, a ball and stumps, commemorating the prowess of Hambledon Cricket Club, 1750–1787. It was unveiled in 1908 in front of 5,000 people after the first match to be played on the site for over 100 years.

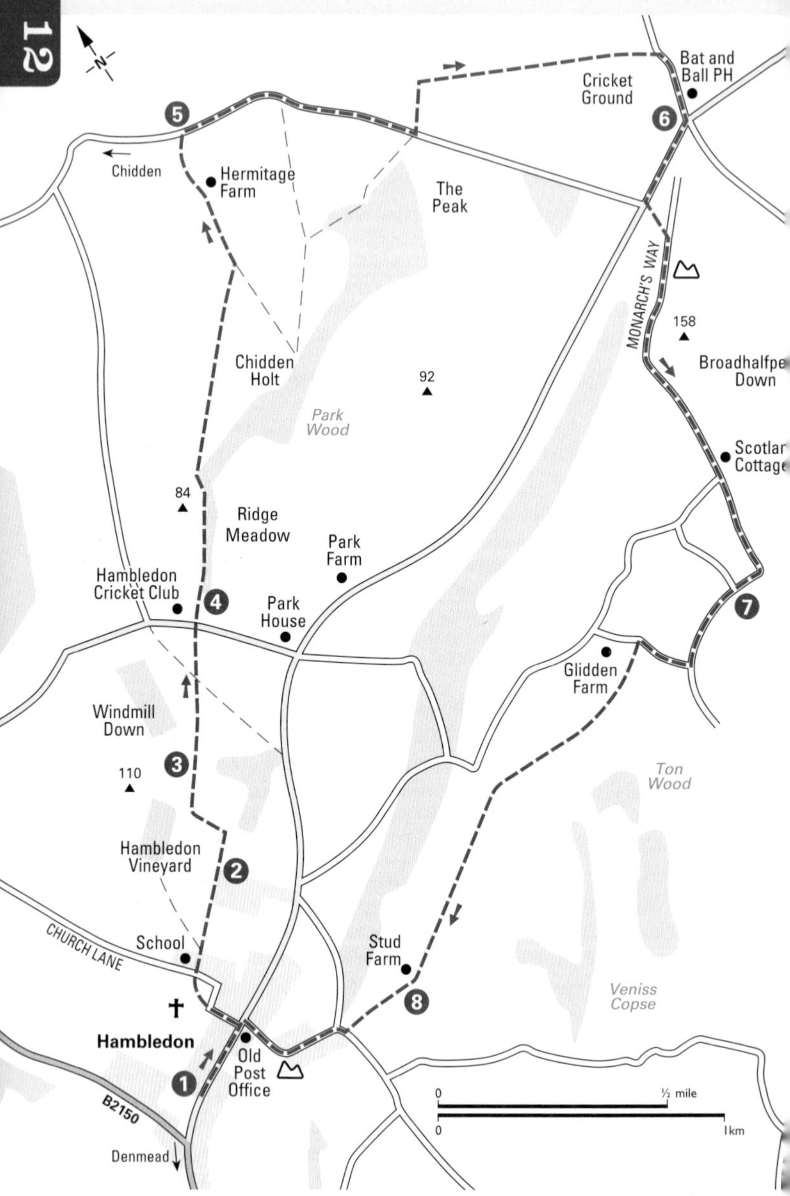


## WALK 12 DIRECTIONS

❶ From the village hall turn left along the street into the centre and turn left opposite the Old Post Office towards the parish church. Follow the public footpath to the right, through the churchyard to Church Lane. Take the road opposite, to the right of the primary school, then, where it turns left, keep ahead along the well waymarked public footpath.

❷ Cross a drive and proceed straight on between the fruit bushes of Hambledon Vineyard. Turn left over a stile; then, after 75yds (69m) carry straight on along the footpath. In 65yds (59m), cross a stile on your right and head towards the right-hand edge of trees opposite.

**WHERE TO EAT AND DRINK**

The famous Bat and Ball pub on Broadhalfpenny Down is open all day and offers Fullers ales and a good selection of bar food. In Hambledon, try the Vine Inn (by the village hall).

❸ Climb a stile and bear right through the trees into a field. Turn left along the field-edge and, in 20yds (18m), bear diagonally right to the corner of a small fenced copse. Continue across the field, heading towards two aerials on the horizon, to cross a road. You are now in Ridge Meadow, the modern home of Hambledon Cricket Club.

❹ Keep to the right-hand edge of the ground and exit in the corner. Cross a field, and continue with woodland on your right. At the end of the woods turn right through the hedge, by a waymarker. Proceed across a large field in a north-easterly direction to a stile. Join a track leading to Hermitage Farm and follow the drive out to the road.

**WHILE YOU'RE THERE**

If you stop for refreshment at the Bat and Ball on Broadhalfpenny Down, look at the collection of cricketing memorabilia, including an inscribed bat presented to Richard Nyren, landlord and greatest all-round cricketer of his day, in 1791.

❺ Turn right for 0.5m (800m) to where a footpath crosses the road. Turn left through the gate and go left around the field-edge to a stile. Turn sharp right along the edge of the next field and continue across two more stiles to a lane. Turn right to the Bat and Ball, cricket ground (with its memorial stone) and crossroads.

❻ Turn right, then in 250yds (229m), opposite the road to Chidden, cross the stile left. Head uphill across the field to a stile and turn right along a track, waymarked 'Monarch's Way'. Follow the track left across Broadhalfpenny Down to Scotland Cottage. Where the drive bears right, keep straight on along a tree-lined path. Gently descend to a track and turn right.

❼ Bear left at a junction; then, in 250yds (229m), turn right along the track to Glidden Farm. Turn left just beyond a pond, bear right at a barn, and keep to the track across fields and stiles. Walk beside power cables, cross a track and bear left to a stile. Cross over a paddock and keep to the left of some fir trees.

❽ Climb a stile to the rear of outbuildings (Stud Farm) on to the access road. Bear off right down a narrow path to a road. Turn right and keep left steeply downhill back into Hambledon. Turn left through the village back to the village hall.

# A Watercress Walk Around the Alresfords

*Exploring the 'new market' town at the heart of Hampshire's watercress industry.*

**DISTANCE** *4 miles (6.4km)* **MINIMUM TIME** *2hrs*
**ASCENT/GRADIENT** *240ft (73m)* ▲▲▲ **LEVEL OF DIFFICULTY** +++
**PATHS** *Riverside paths, tracks, field, woodland paths and roads*
**LANDSCAPE** *River valley and undulating farmland dotted with woodland*
**SUGGESTED MAP** *OS Explorer 132 Winchester*
**START / FINISH** *Grid reference: SU 588325*
**DOG FRIENDLINESS** *Keep dogs under control*
**PARKING** *Pay-and-display car park off Station Road, New Alresford*
**PUBLIC TOILETS** *New Alresford*

New Alresford (pronounced Allsford) is not very new at all. In fact, this delightful place, one of Hampshire's most picturesque small towns, was 'new' in 1200, when Godfrey de Lucy, Bishop of Winchester, wanted to expand the original Alresford – Old Alresford. He dammed the River Arle, creating a 200-acre (81ha) pond, and built a causeway (the Great Weir) to link Old Alresford with his new community. His 'New Market', as it was first called, thrived to become a prosperous wool town, with a market being held in Broad Street.

## Georgian Architecture

Most of the medieval timber-framed houses were destroyed by two devastating fires during the 17th century, one in 1644 when the Royalists set the town alight following the Battle of Cheriton. As a result, much of the architecture is Georgian, notably along sumptuous Broad Street which is lined with limes and elegant colour-washed houses. Mary Russell Mitford, the authoress of *Our Village* which sketches her country life, was born in Broad Street in 1787.

Close to both Old and New Alresford you will find an intricate network of crystal clear chalk streams, rivulets and channels that form the rivers Arle and Itchen and the Candover Stream. Since Victorian times these springs and rivers have played a vital role in one of Alresford's major industries, the production of watercress. Surprisingly, watercress never stops growing in the spring water that emanates from the ground at a constant 51 degrees Fahrenheit throughout the year. These ideal growing conditions made Alresford the 'Watercress Capital' of England, with the railway providing the vital link for the industry, transporting watercress to London and much of the country. The watercress beds continue to thrive in this health-conscious age.

You'll pass several watercress beds where you can see how the water is collected in concrete channels and pumped back up again. You'll also pass the impressive, 300-year-old, thatched and timber-framed Fulling Mill which straddles the River Arle. Here, home-spun wool was scoured,

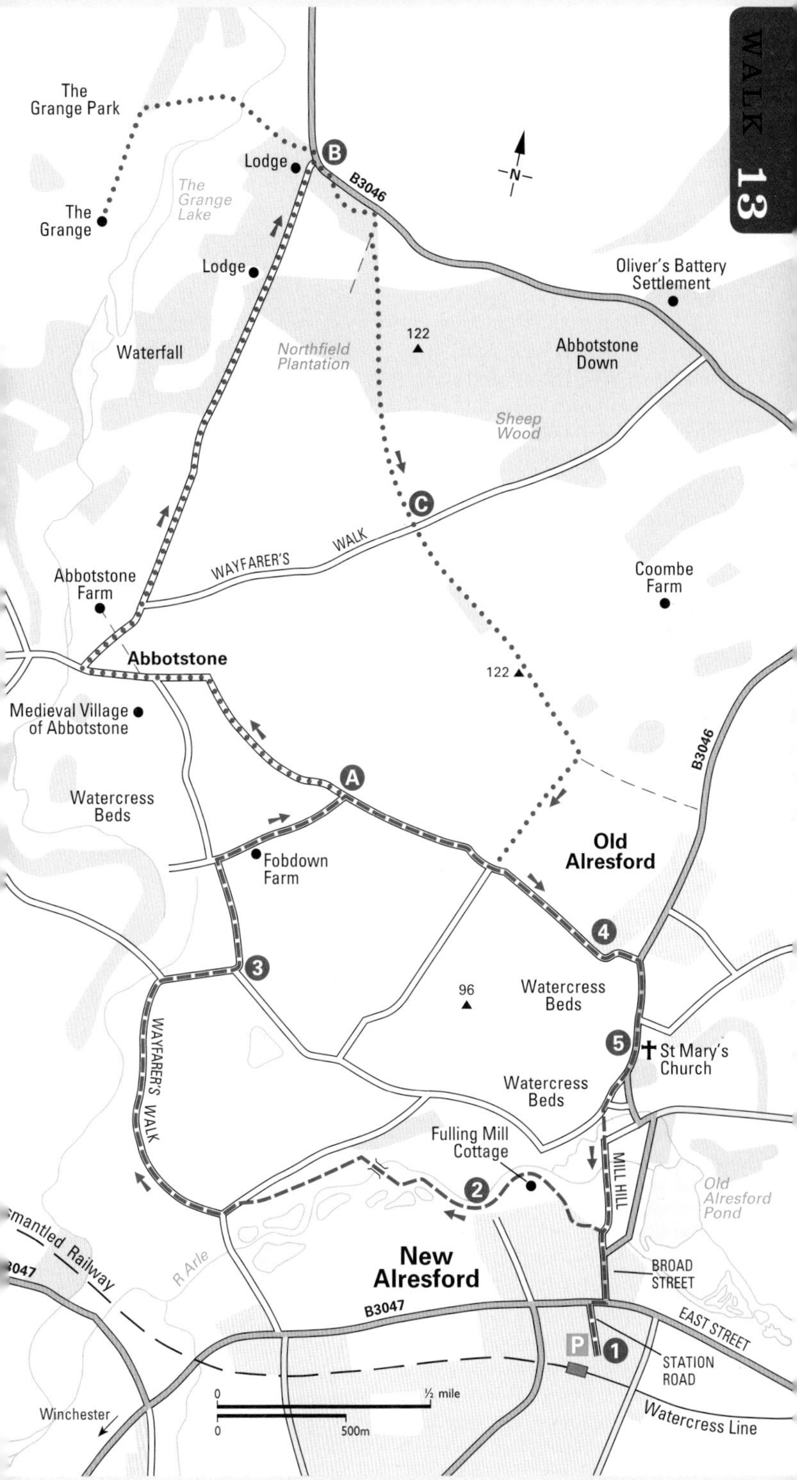

The Grange Park
The Grange
Lodge
The Grange Lake
B
B3046
N
Lodge
Oliver's Battery Settlement
122
Waterfall
Northfield Plantation
Abbotstone Down
Sheep Wood
C
WAYFARER'S WALK
Abbotstone Farm
Coombe Farm
Abbotstone
122
Medieval Village of Abbotstone
B3046
A
Watercress Beds
Fobdown Farm
Old Alresford
4
3
96
Watercress Beds
5
St Mary's Church
WAYFARER'S WALK
Watercress Beds
Fulling Mill Cottage
MILL HILL
Old Alresford Pond
2
Dismantled Railway
B3047
R Arle
New Alresford
BROAD STREET
B3047
EAST STREET
P
1
STATION ROAD
0
½ mile
0
500m
Winchester
Watercress Line

washed, pounded with mallets, stretched, dried, brushed and sheared. Old Alresford is tiny, with an interesting 18th-century church and two substantial Georgian houses. Make time to visit the church to see the striking monument to Jane Rodney. Admiral Lord Rodney, who is buried in the family vault, built Old Alresford House and is famous for spectacularly defeating the Spanish fleet off Cape St Vincent in 1780.

## WALK 13 DIRECTIONS

1 From the car park walk down Station Road to the T-junction with West Street. Turn right, then left down Broad Street and keep left at the bottom along Mill Hill. Half way down turn left into Ladywell Lane and soon join the river bank and pass the attractive, timbered and thatched Fulling Mill Cottage which straddles the River Arle.

2 Continue to the bottom of Dean Lane and keep to the riverside path. Cross a footbridge over the river, and ascend to pass some cottages. Shortly, a lane merges from your right; follow it for 50yds (46m), then fork right onto the Wayfarer's Walk and continue to a junction of tracks. Bear right uphill to a lane.

3 Turn left, descend to Fobdown Farm and take the track on the right beside the farm buildings. On reaching a T-junction of tracks, turn right and follow the established track for just over 0.5mile (800m), gently descending into Old Alresford.

### WHERE TO EAT AND DRINK

The Globe in New Alresford offers good pub food, decent ale and wine, and views across Alresford Pond from its waterside garden. Alternatively, try the Horse and Groom or, for good light lunches and teas, Tiffins Tea Room, at the bottom of West Street.

### WHAT TO LOOK OUT FOR

Note the Old Sun, a former pub, in East Street, where John Arlott, the cricket commentator and writer, lived. In the churchyard you'll find the graves of French prisoners of war, who died in the village while on parole during the Napoleonic Wars. More unusually, the grave of a stray dog called Hambone Junior can be found close to the River Arle. It was adopted by American soldiers waiting at Alresford for the D-Day invasion in June 1944 but was run over and killed.

4 Pass watercress beds on your right and follow the now metalled lane left, past houses. Turn right beside the green to reach the B3046. Cross over and follow the pavement right to a lane opposite St Mary's Church.

5 Having visited the church, cross the road and turn left along the pavement to a grass triangle by a junction. Bear right along the lane and take the footpath ahead over a stream and beside watercress beds back to Mill Hill and Broad Street.

### WHILE YOU'RE THERE

Enjoy a steam train ride on the Watercress Line between New Alresford and Alton. It was from here that watercress was transported to London and there are four stations, sheds and special events.



*Right: Alresford (Walk 13)*

# The Grange at Northington

*From New Alresford to a stunning neo-classical mansion.*

**See map and information panel for Walk 13**

DISTANCE *9 miles (14.5km)* MINIMUM TIME *4hrs*

ASCENT/GRADIENT *656ft (200m)* ▲▲▲ LEVEL OF DIFFICULTY +++

## WALK 14 DIRECTIONS (Walk 13 option)

You can extend your walk into the countryside around Alresford and see the majestic ruin of The Grange. At the T-junction of tracks above Fobdown Farm, Point Ⓐ, turn left and keep to the track for 0.5 mile (800m) to a lane.

Just before you reach the lane, the field on your left hides the site of the medieval village of Abbotstone. Covering some 15 acres (6ha), it was once a flourishing community with a manor, church and mill, and wealthy enough to be taxed in 1327. You can see earthworks and depressions representing outlines of streets and houses.

Bear right, then right again along a track towards Abbotstone Farm. Keep ahead at the first junction, then ignore the waymarked track right (Wayfarer's Walk), and proceed ahead on the track. This becomes metalled and in 0.5 mile (800m) descends to a lodge and the entrance to The Grange, Point Ⓑ. Follow the drive for 0.25 mile (400m) to visit this fine building, then return to the lodge. The Grange is an important house architecturally, being designed in 1804 by William Wilkins, architect of the National Gallery, in the Greek Revivalist style. The majestic building looks more like a Greek temple with a Parthenon-like portico supported by two rows of giant Doric columns. It commands a superb position overlooking a wonderfully peaceful landscape, including a lake and rolling parkland.

At the B3046, turn right and immediately go through a kissing gate by the bus shelter into woodland. Continue through a second gate then cross a driveway and follow the path beside the drive. Bear right alongside woodland to a track by a house. Turn left, enter rough grassland and bear right, following the narrow path into Northfield Plantation. Keep ahead on merging with a track. Leave the wood and descend along the field-edge to a crossing of paths by a derelict barn (Point Ⓒ). Proceed ahead up the right-hand field-edge to a gap in the hedge and follow the grassy path between fields. Turn on to a permissive path on your right 120yds (110m) beyond a metal barn and walk along the field-edge to a crossing of tracks. Turn left down to Old Alresford rejoining Walk 13 at Point ❹.

*Right: Northington Grange (Walk 14)*

SILCHESTER

# Exploring Roman Calleva

*Revealing the history of this Roman town and its impressive surviving walls.*

**DISTANCE** *4.25 miles (6.8km)* **MINIMUM TIME** *2hrs*
**ASCENT/GRADIENT** *171ft (52m)* ▲▲▲ **LEVEL OF DIFFICULTY** +++
**PATHS** *Field paths and woodland tracks, 9 stiles*
**LANDSCAPE** *Open farmland, mixed woodland*
**SUGGESTED MAP** *OS Explorer 159 Reading, Wokingham & Pangbourne*
**START / FINISH** *Grid reference: SU 643623*
**DOG FRIENDLINESS** *Let them run free in Benyon's Inclosure*
**PARKING** *Church of St Mary the Virgin, Silchester*
**PUBLIC TOILETS** *None en route*

## WALK 15 DIRECTIONS

Tucked away between Basingstoke and Reading is a pocket of gently undulating countryside. Here you will find stretches of ancient woodland, open farmland and a web of narrow, leafy lanes leading to isolated farms, secluded villages, stately houses, and the fascinating site of the Roman town of Calleva Atrebatum.

The walk begins by the impressive defensive walls and you should allow time to pause at the information boards dotted around the Town Trail. These offer more detail on the town's development and explain how the encircling walls were built. From the church, turn right along the road and bear off right to follow the Town Trail beside or along the top of the perimeter wall where possible. At the South Gate, go outside the wall and follow the path through woods to the left of the wall.

Calleva was already the prosperous tribal capital of Atrebates and an administrative centre for a large area before the Romans developed the site following the invasion in AD 43. It became a key military and commercial centre and important roads radiated from it. Earth ramparts were built to protect the buildings between AD 160 and 200 and the facing walls which you see today were added between AD 250 and 275. The wall, 1.25 miles (2km) round, enclosed broad streets laid out at right angles, great buildings and villas.

The site was thoroughly excavated during Victorian times, exposing a partial plan, including a road network, foundations of buildings, and what has been interpreted as the earliest known Christian church in Britain. More recent

### WHAT TO LOOK OUT FOR

A visit to the Church of St Mary the Virgin, which dates from 1180 and features Roman bricks incorporated into the walls and buttresses, will reveal simple, 13th-century wall paintings and an organ from about 1770.

WHERE TO EAT AND DRINK

Half-way round you will find the Red Lion, an attractive pub dating from 1575, with a flower-filled front terrace, a beamed bar with log fires in winter, real ales and an extensive bar menu.

excavations have revealed that Calleva was probably occupied until the 6th or 7th centuries AD and did not decline in the 5th century as earlier evidence seemed to suggest. Today, you can see little of the town above ground as the buildings were re-buried to protect them from the weather, vegetation, vandals and souvenir hunters.

Half way round, go through a gate and turn left along the track through a second gate. Follow the footpath across a stile and continue to a metalled lane. Turn right, then right again at the junction and almost immediately turn left, signed towards Tadley. Turn right along a gravel track, passing beside a gate into woodland. Turn right at a crossing by a green Englefield Estate sign, following the path downhill to a fork. Keep left and cross the causeway beside the lake. Where the path curves left, keep right uphill, following a narrow woodland path. Keep ahead across a track, a few paces from a gate on your right, and descend into thicker woods to cross a stream.

Having strolled around the Roman walls, the walk takes you into Benyon's Inclosure, peaceful mixed woodlands that were once part of Pamber Forest, an ancient forest where King John is reputed to have hunted deer.

Keep right to cross a boardwalk and head uphill to a barrier and a road. Turn right, pass the Red Lion, then take the second track on the left. Cross a bridge and follow the byway uphill. As it curves right and levels out, look out for the yellow marker on a post on the left. Take the footpath left through the edge of a copse to a stile and proceed ahead, keeping left along the field-edge to a stile. Cross a farm track and the stile opposite, then keep to the left-hand hedge to a stile in the field corner and then cross another track and stiles.

Continue ahead along the edge of the field, following it to the left until you reach a gate and stile on your right. Fork right over the stile, walking diagonally across the field to a stile by a water trough. Proceed straight ahead to cross a stile beside an oak tree and pass under power cables. Continue for 100yds (91m) and turn right to a stile. Continue downhill to a plank bridge and a stile. Gently ascend the field and merge with a track, then join a metalled drive leading to a lane. On your right is a gate leading to the amphitheatre. Walk ahead along the lane, turning right to the church.

WHILE YOU'RE THERE

Visit Reading Museum to see the Silchester Collection, a wealth of items from the Roman town. Most were found during excavations of the area between 1890 and 1909.

Just off your route is the recently excavated Roman amphitheatre. Built in the 1st century AD, it could accommodate over 4,000 spectators on wooden seats above the walls. Here the citizens came to watch sports, gladiatorial contests and public executions.

# Meon Valley Meander

*Rising dramatically above the Meon Valley, Old Winchester Hill is a favoured haunt of historians and naturalists.*

**DISTANCE** *6.75 miles (10.9km)* **MINIMUM TIME** *3hrs 30min*

**ASCENT/GRADIENT** *472ft (144m)* ▲▲▲ **LEVEL OF DIFFICULTY** +++

**PATHS** *Field paths, footpaths, tracks and sections of road, 7 stiles*

**LANDSCAPE** *Chalk downland, gently rolling farmland and river valley*

**SUGGESTED MAP** *OS Explorer 119 Meon Valley*

**START / FINISH** *Grid reference: SU 645214*

**DOG FRIENDLINESS** *Let them off lead on old railway path*

**PARKING** *Natural England car park off Old Winchester Hill Lane*

**PUBLIC TOILETS** *None en route*

Old Winchester Hill dominates the Meon Valley. From its summit, some 646ft (197m) above sea level, you can savour far-reaching views across the Solent to the Isle of Wight, west to the New Forest and Wiltshire, and north to Beacon Hill. It's long been a natural vantage point, attracting early settlers who preferred the safety afforded by the high ground. The impressive remains of the fort you see today on the summit date back to the Iron Age. Its defences comprise a massive single bank and ditch enclosing about 14 acres (4ha) with entrances at the east and west ends. The oval-shaped fort overlies a pattern of prehistoric fields and you will notice some large grassy mounds as you walk round the rampart. These are Bronze Age burial mounds, erected on the crest of the hill between 4,500 and 3,500 years ago for important members of society.

## Nature Reserve

Old Winchester Hill was purchased by the state in 1954 and is now a National Nature Reserve, cared for by Natural England. The sheep-grazed chalk downland, with its mix of open grassland, scrub and woodland, is home to a number of rare butterflies and chalk-loving flowers. Walk this way in early summer and you will see the hill-fort dotted with fragrant orchids, while in July look out for the bright blue round-headed rampion, a rarity in Britain, but which thrives here. On a warm August day the grassland is a sea of colour with hundreds of plants, flowers and wild herbs. In fact, an area just 1m (3ft) square can contain 30–40 different species of plant and over 200 species have been recorded on the reserve. The air shimmers with thousands of chalkhill blue butterflies, feeding on the wild majoram, the plants on the reserve providing food for some 34 species of butterfly and their caterpillars. The longer grass is favoured by hedge and meadow browns and the beautiful marbled white butterflies. Bring your binoculars, and you may see a peregrine falcon hunting, buzzards soaring high on the thermals, and summer migrants like the redstart and pied flycatcher. In winter, fieldfares and redwings feed in numbers on the abundant juniper berries, while the yew woods provide shelter to titmice and goldcrests.

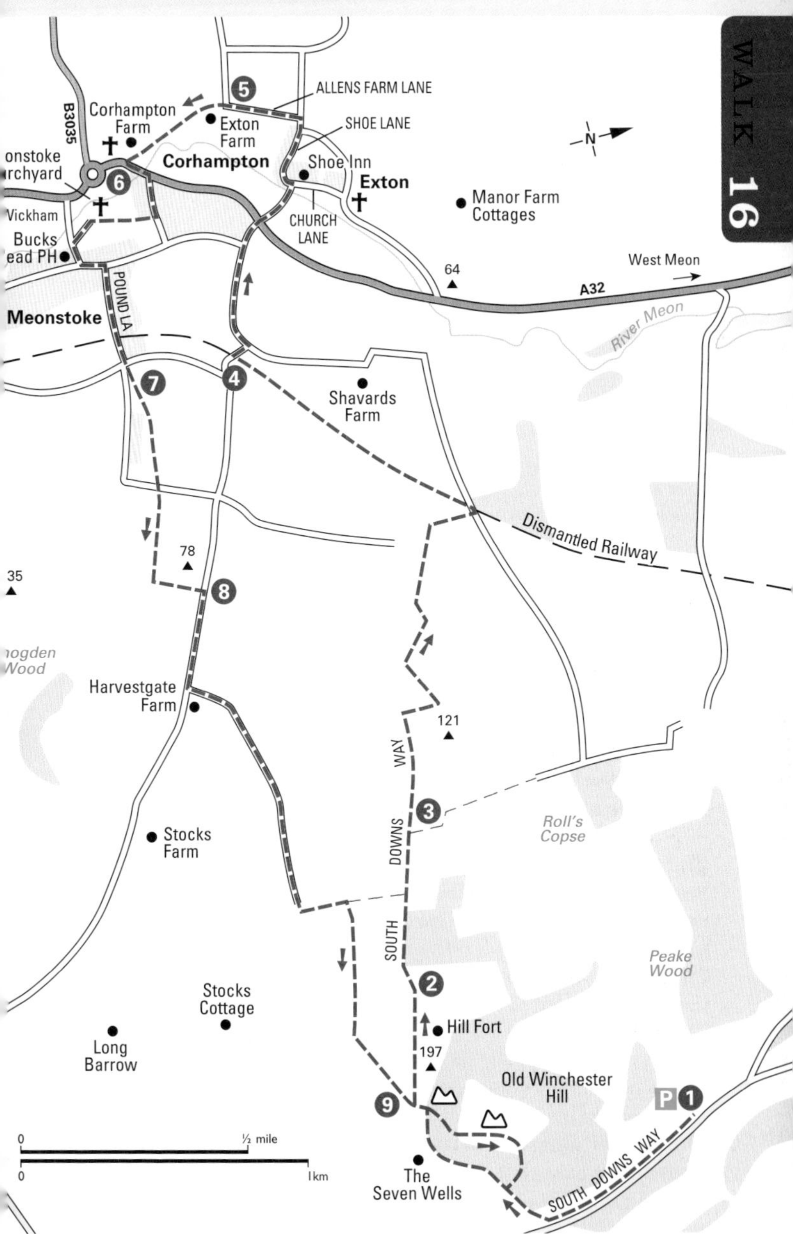


## WALK 16 DIRECTIONS

❶ From the car park go through the gate onto the open downland and turn left, leaving the information board on your right. Follow the path around the perimeter of the reserve, merge with the South Downs Way (SDW) and bear right towards the hill-fort. Pass through a gate, following SDW markers left, then right, across the centre of the fort.

❷ Descend through the ramparts, heading downhill

to a gate. Pass beneath yew trees and beside a gate; then, when the path swings right at a fingerpost, keep ahead along the SDW.

❸ Follow the enclosed path downhill to reach a junction of paths; cross the footbridge and turn left, following the signposted 'SDW'. Climb the steps on to the former Meon Valley railway, and turn left along the old line for just over 0.5 mile (800m).

**WHERE TO EAT AND DRINK**

There's a friendly welcome, a riverside garden and good food at the Bucks Head (open all day at weekends).

❹ Drop down to a lane, turn right under the missing bridge, then immediately left at the junction. Walk along Stocks Lane to the A32 and carefully cross the main road into Beacon Hill Lane. Turn left just before the Shoe Inn, and shortly bear left along Allens Farm Lane.

❺ At a sharp right-hand bend, keep ahead along the path beside Exton Farm. Go through a gate and bear left between paddocks to a stile. Pass beside Corhampton Farm and Church, bearing left to the A32.

❻ Cross, turn left along the pavement and right by the shop. Take the metalled path beside the last house on your right and enter Meonstoke churchyard. Turn left along the lane to a T-junction beside the Bucks Head. Turn left, then left again at the junction. Follow the lane right (Pound Lane) to cross the old railway.

**WHILE YOU'RE THERE**

Visit St John's churchyard in West Meon. Here you'll find the graves of Thomas Lord, the founder of Lord's cricket ground, who retired to the village in 1830, and Guy Burgess, the former British diplomat and Russian agent who died in Moscow in 1963.

❼ At a crossroads climb the stile on your left. Proceed ahead across the field and pass behind gardens, eventually reaching a stile and a lane. Climb the stile opposite and keep to the right-hand field-edge to a stile. Maintain direction to a stile, then bear diagonally left towards a house and road.

❽ Turn right and take the track left beside Harvestgate Farm. At the top of the track, bear left uphill along the field-edge, then sharp right, following the bridleway along the hedge into the next field. Turn through a kissing gate on your left into the Nature Reserve and ascend steeply to the hill fort ramparts.

❾ Bear right to join the outward route by the fort entrance. Turn left to walk down the steps beside a seat and information board, and then continue to follow a path just beneath the downland rim. Bear right to a gate and retrace your steps to the car park.

**WHAT TO LOOK OUT FOR**

Corhampton Church is remarkable in having no dedication, and has remained almost unaltered since it was built in the11th century. Many Saxon details can be seen, including 'long and short' stonework at the corners. Note too the sundial on the south wall (divided into eight sections not twelve), the 12th-century wall paintings in the chancel, a 1000-year-old yew tree and the Romano-British coffin in the churchyard.

# Tichborne Family Traditions

*A gentle walk across a Civil War battlefield and through the Itchen Valley.*



**DISTANCE** *6.5 miles (10.4km)* **MINIMUM TIME** *3hrs*

**ASCENT/GRADIENT** *426ft (130m)* ▲▲▲ **LEVEL OF DIFFICULTY** +++

**PATHS** *Field paths, downland tracks and some road walking*

**LANDSCAPE** *River valley and undulating farmland dotted with woodland*

**SUGGESTED MAP** *OS Explorer 132 Winchester*

**START / FINISH** *Grid reference: SU 583286*

**DOG FRIENDLINESS** *Keep dogs under control*

**PARKING** *Cheriton. Roadside parking on village lane east of B3046*

**PUBLIC TOILETS** *None en route*

Tiny Tichborne is idyllic. Thatched and timber-framed cottages line the lane winding up to St Andrew's Church, handsome farms and the magnificent manor house nestle close to the infant River Itchen in a valley setting. This is perfect walking country and this gentle ramble incorporates two of Hampshire's long distance trails, the Itchen Way and the Wayfarers Walk, as it wends its way to the unspoilt and intriguing estate village which has been dominated by the Tichborne family for over nine centuries.

## Oldest Seat

The manor has been the seat of the Tichbornes, the oldest family in Hampshire, since 1135 when Henry de Blois, Bishop of Winchester, granted part of his estate to Walter de Tichborne. A manor house has stood by the river since the 13th century, although the present building dates from 1803. There can hardly be a family with a more colourful and, at times, tragic history in England, for the Tichbornes and the village are famous for the tradition of the Tichborne Dole and the trial of the Tichborne Claimant.

The Tichborne Dole is one of the oldest surviving traditions in Britain. It's said that in the 13th century Lady Mabella Tichborne, wife of Sir Roger Tichborne, decided on her deathbed that she should provide a 'dole' of bread for the poor of the parish to be distributed on Lady Day, 25th March. Sir Roger, who was not a charitable man, reluctantly granted her request for a piece of land to ensure that the dole would continue after her death. However, there was one condition. He told her she could have as much land as she could get around unaided, while a firebrand stayed alight. Although weak and unable to walk, she managed to crawl around 23 acres (9.3ha) of land which, even today, is known as 'The Crawls'. He kept his promise and to this day every parishioner of Tichborne and Cheriton receives a gallon of flour when they assemble at Tichborne House on Lady Day.

The Tichborne family were involved in another notable controversy during the 19th century, that of the Tichborne Claimant, which caused one of the longest trials in Victorian England. Another Roger Tichborne was presumed lost at sea en route to South America in 1854, but his mother never gave up hope of seeing him again and she placed adverts in the press offering a reward for the discovery of her missing son. Eventually, in 1872, a man arrived from Australia claiming to be her son. Even at 24 stone (173kg) and in middle age (Roger was younger and slim), he convinced the mother that he was her son and they swore affidavits before she died. The family contested his claim to the family fortune and the ensuing Tichborne Claimant case lasted ten months. Eventually Arthur Orton, a Wapping butcher, was jailed for 14 years but the action cost the family £80,000.

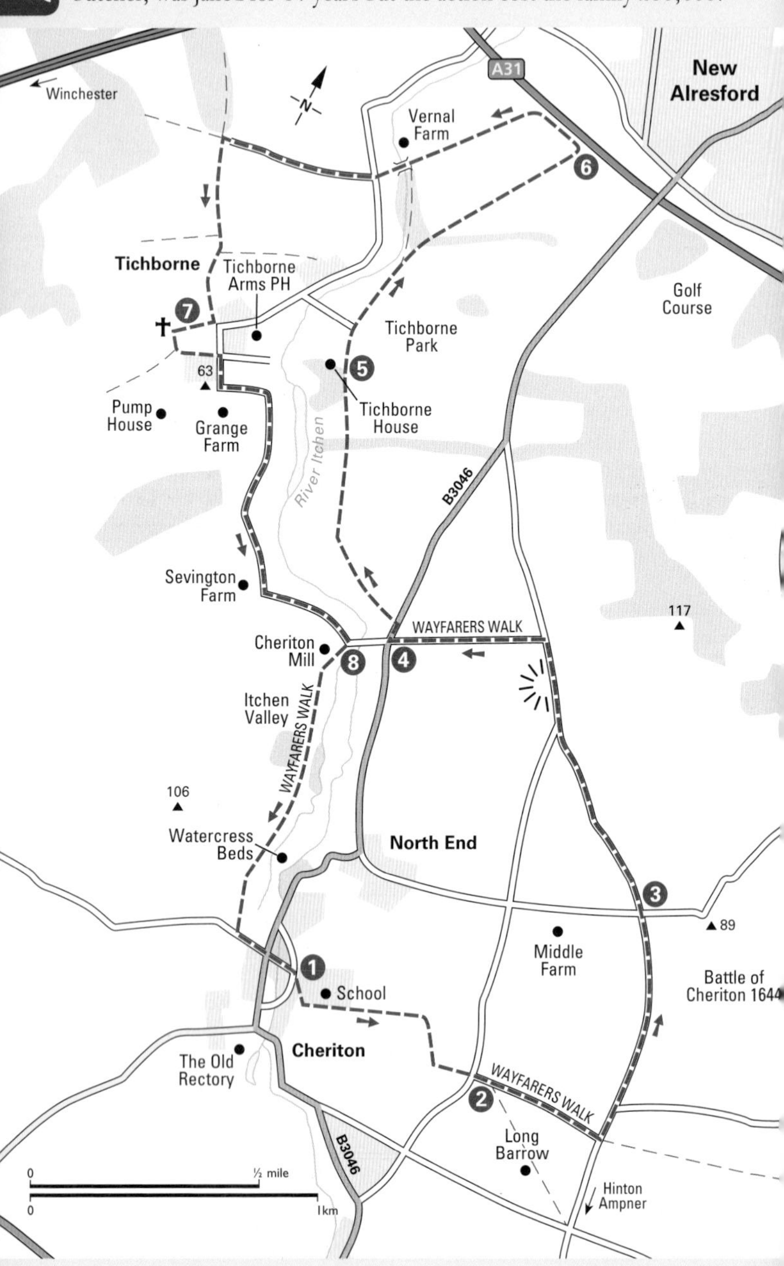

## WALK 17 DIRECTIONS

1 From the village lane, cross the small brick bridge close to Freeman's Yard and bear right in front of the school. Just beyond a house (Martyrwell), turn left along a narrow fenced path and climb out of the village to a stile. Turn right around the field-edge to a stile and crossing of paths.

**WHERE TO EAT AND DRINK**

The thatched Tichborne Arms offers home-made food, real ale and a garden. In Cheriton, post-walk refreshment can be enjoyed at the Flower Pots, noted for its home-brewed beers, bar food and warm welcome.

2 Proceed straight ahead along the grassy track to a crossing of routes. The fields in the shallow valley away to your left were the site of the Battle of Cheriton in 1644. Turn left downhill and keep to the track to a lane by a barn.

3 Cross the lane and walk along the farm track. A track merges from the left, beyond which you climb to a junction of paths. With lovely views across the Itchen Valley, turn left downhill, following the track to the B3046.

**WHILE YOU'RE THERE**

Just south of Cheriton is Hinton Ampner, a Georgian house, owned by the National Trust and displaying a fine collection of Regency furniture and Italian paintings. You could also drive to grid ref 600303, east of Cheriton, to find the Cheriton Battlefield commemorative stone. This is the site of a violent and decisive Civil War battle in March 1644, when 2,000 men were slain as the Parliamentarians defeated the Royalists.

4 Turn right then, after 70yds (64m), cross the road and take the path left, across the field parallel with the river. Cross a stile and proceed to a gate on the edge of a copse. Walk through the trees, cross the stile and keep to the left-hand edge of pasture (Tichborne House is to the left) to a stile by the drive entrance.

5 Turn right, keep ahead then, where the metalled estate road curves left, proceed along a track. Just before you reach some woodland, bear off right along a grassy track into a field. Bear half right, walking diagonally across the field and gently uphill to meet a bridleway above the A31.

6 Turn left (signed 'Itchen Way'), pass Vernal Farm, then cross the River Itchen to a lane. Take the path opposite, uphill along the field-edge. In the top left-hand corner, follow the track left into a field. Turn left along the field-edge, downhill towards Tichborne church. Ignore tracks right and left and continue to the village lane (the Tichborne Arms is to the left here).

7 Just before the lane, take the path right uphill to the church. On leaving the church, follow the access lane downhill to a T-junction. Turn right and follow the lane for a mile (1.6km), close to Tichborne Park and the river, to Cheriton Mill.

8 Follow the Wayfarers Walk right, beside the mill to a gate. Walk in front of a cottage to a stile and continue ahead parallel with the river. Cross double stiles and maintain direction to a stile by a gate. Continue to a gate and turn left along the lane to the B3046 in Cheriton. Cross over to reach the village lane and your car.

# Alfred's Ancient Capital

*Winchester's historic streets, Cathedral Close and the beautiful Itchen Valley.*

**DISTANCE** *4 miles (6.4km)* **MINIMUM TIME** *2hrs*

**ASCENT/GRADIENT** *499ft (152m)* ▲▲▲ **LEVEL OF DIFFICULTY** +++

**PATHS** *Established riverside paths through water-meadows, 3 stiles*

**LANDSCAPE** *City streets, riverside, water-meadow and downland*

**SUGGESTED MAP** *OS Explorer 132 Winchester*

**START / FINISH** *Grid reference: SU 485294*

**DOG FRIENDLINESS** *Under control through water-meadows and by golf course*

**PARKING** *Pay-and-display car parks in city centre*

**PUBLIC TOILETS** *The Broadway, Winchester*

Historic Winchester, ancient capital of Wessex and England, was first settled in the Iron Age and influenced by royalty since the 7th century, the city boasts some remarkable architectural treasures.

Beginning from the imposing bronze statue of King Alfred the Great, who made the city his capital, you have the choice of two walks. The shorter Walk 18 incorporates some of the famous sights, with a stroll through the water-meadows to the Hospital of St Cross and St Catherine's Hill. The longer Walk 19 follows the Itchen Valley and returns to Winchester across Twyford Down, with its glorious views across the city.

From the Victorian Guildhall, you walk up the High Street, which has been a main thoroughfare to a crossing point on the River Itchen for some 2,500 years, before reaching the Cathedral Close. The magnificent cathedral was founded in 1079 on the site of an earlier Saxon building and remodelled in the 14th century. It is the longest medieval church in Europe and among its treasures are the 12th-century illuminated Winchester Bible, medieval wall paintings and the tombs of early English kings and more recent notables, including Jane Austen and Izaak Walton.

In the close you will find half-timbered Cheyney Court, formerly the Bishop's court house. Beyond Kingsgate you'll pass the entrance to Winchester College, founded in 1382 by William of Wykeham, the oldest school in England. Join one of the guided tours (in summer only) to view the handsome courtyards and cloisters, the chapel with its early 16th-century stained-glass window, and to savour the unspoilt medieval atmosphere. At the end of College Street you'll see the Bishops of Winchester's house, the surviving wing of a grand palace built in 1684 overlooking the striking ruins of the 12th-century Wolvesey Palace.

Set in the wide, lush water-meadows beside the Itchen, at the end of the beautiful riverside walk beside the College grounds, is the Hospital of St Cross. Founded in 1132, it still functions as an almshouse and is the oldest charitable institution in the country. Here you can visit the fine Norman church, the Brethrens Hall and medieval kitchen, and take the 'Wayfarer's Dole' – bread and ale – a tradition that survives from the Middle Ages.

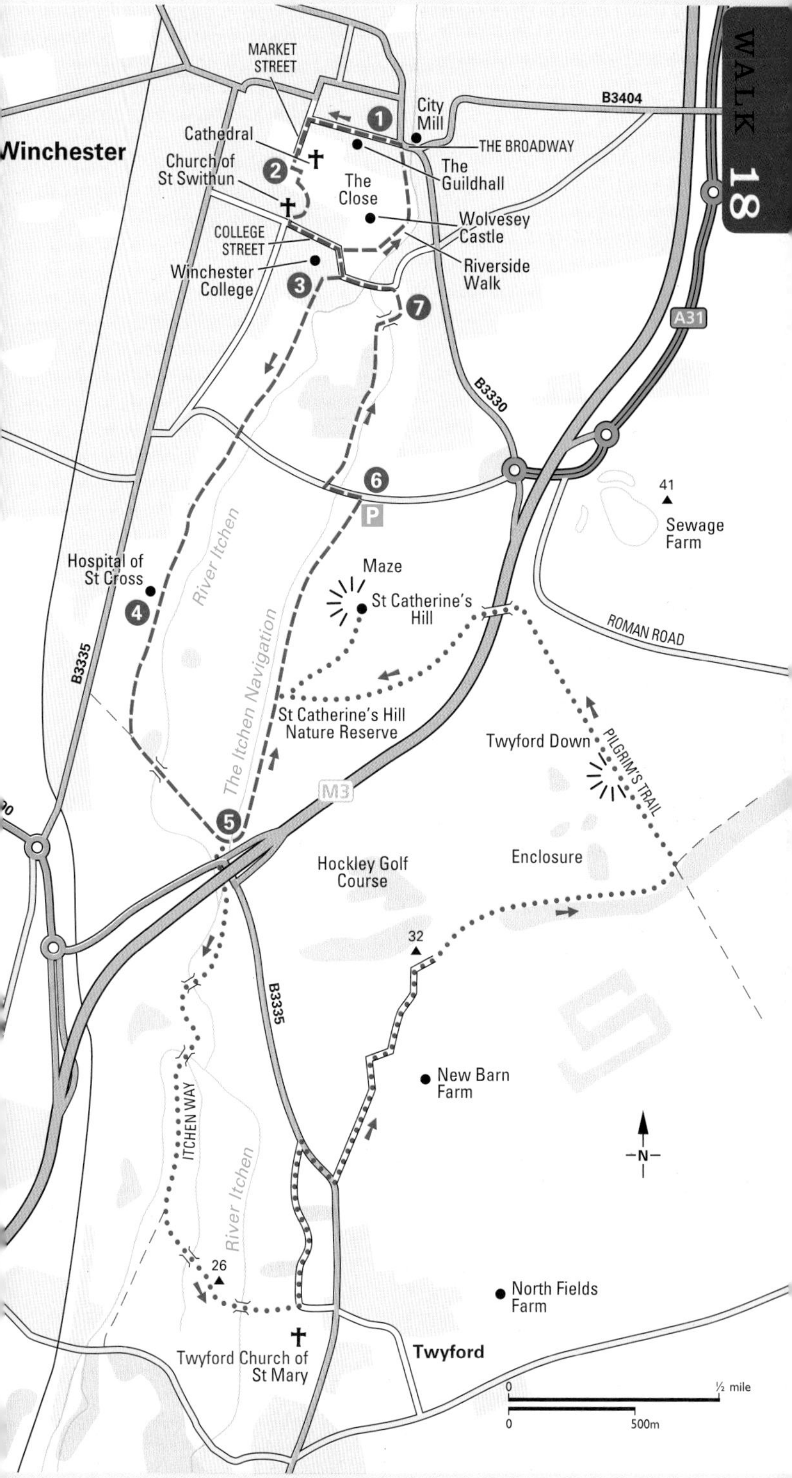

MARKET STREET
City Mill
B3404
Winchester
Cathedral
THE BROADWAY
Church of St Swithun
The Close
The Guildhall
Wolvesey Castle
COLLEGE STREET
Winchester College
Riverside Walk
A31
B3330
41
Sewage Farm
River Itchen
Hospital of St Cross
Maze
St Catherine's Hill
ROMAN ROAD
The Itchen Navigation
B3335
St Catherine's Hill Nature Reserve
Twyford Down
PILGRIM'S TRAIL
M3
Hockley Golf Course
Enclosure
32
B3335
New Barn Farm
ITCHEN WAY
River Itchen
N
26
North Fields Farm
Twyford Church of St Mary
Twyford
0 ½ mile
0 500m

## WALK 18 DIRECTIONS

❶ From King Alfred's statue on the Broadway, walk towards the city centre, passing the Guildhall (tourist information centre) on your left. Join the High Street, then in 100yds (91m), turn left along Market Street. Continue ahead on to Cathedral Green to pass the cathedral's main door.

❷ Turn left down a cloister (signed to Wolvesey Castle), then right through the Close, to Cheyney Court and exit via Prior's Gate. Turn left though Kingsgate, with the tiny Church of St Swithun above, then turn left down College Street and shortly pass the entrance to Winchester College. Beyond the road barrier, turn right along College Walk, then turn right at the end of the wall, along a college access road.

❸ Go left by a private entrance to the college. Follow the path beside the River Itchen for 0.5 mile (800m) to a gate and road bridge. Cross over and follow the riverside gravel path to a gate and cross open meadow towards the Hosptial of St Cross.

❹ Keep left alongside the wall and through an avenue of trees to a stile. Keep ahead on the gravel path to two further stiles and join a farm track leading to a traffic-free lane. Turn left and continue across the River Itchen to reach a junction of metalled paths by the M3.

❺ Turn left along a path. Go under an old railway and pass a gate on your right (access to St Catherine's Hill and where Walk 19 merges). Keep left at a fork and drop down to follow a narrow path by the Itchen Navigation. Go through the car park to the road.

❻ Turn left across the bridge and take the footpath immediately right. Keep to the path beside the water, disregarding the path left (College nature reserve). Soon cross the bridge by rowing sheds to join a metalled track.

❼ Turn left, then left again at the road. Follow it right along College Walk and turn right at the end on to a metalled path. Pass the Old Bishops Palace (Wolvesey Castle) and follow the path beside the Itchen to Bridge Street, opposite the National Trust's City Mill. Turn left to King Alfred's statue.

### WHAT TO LOOK OUT FOR

St Catherine's Hill, Winchester's most prominent landmark, is well worth the detour as you head back into the city. It was the site of the area's first settlement and on its summit are the rampart and ditch of an Iron Age hill fort, the Norman remains of St Catherine's Chapel, and a 17th-century turf-cut maze. You'll also be rewarded with excellent views of the city.

### WHERE TO EAT AND DRINK

Old pubs, tea rooms and restaurants abound around the cathedral and its close. Try the excellent Cathedral Refectory or the Courtyard Café behind the Guildhall, or the Wykeham Arms, in Kingsgate Street.

### WHILE YOU'RE THERE

Allow time to visit Winchester's City Museum on the edge of the Cathedral Green. It tells the story of the city, as an important Roman town and the principal city of King Alfred, through Anglo-Saxon and Norman England to modern times.

# Twyford Down

*A longer loop takes in some of the Itchen Valley and Twyford Down.*

**See map and information panel for Walk 18**



**DISTANCE** *8 miles (12.9km)* **MINIMUM TIME** *4hrs*

**ASCENT/GRADIENT** *499ft (152m)* ▲▲▲ **LEVEL OF DIFFICULTY** +++

**PATHS** *Town trail then field paths and downland tracks, 5 stiles*

## WALK 19 DIRECTIONS (Walk 18 option)

After Point 5, the end of the gated road, turn right towards Twyford and cross at the lights. Turn right along the pavement, soon forking left under the M3 alongside the Itchen Navigation.

The Itchen Navigation, a canalised section of the river, was established in the 17th century. It was used to transport heavy cargoes such as coal in horse-drawn barges from Southampton docks to Wharf Hill in Winchester. It included 15 locks and you can see the remains of these as you follow the Itchen Way.

Keep beside the river, crossing a bridge, sluices and stiles. At the second footbridge across the river, bear left past a bench and through a kissing gate into meadow. Cross a bridge and bear half right towards Twyford church. Cross a footbridge, go through a gate and follow the left-hand fence to a gate and cross the river. At the road junction, turn left (the church is on the right), and follow the lane to the B3335.

Twyford's Church of St Mary, re-built in 1878, is worth closer inspection for the historical village notes, in particular the romantic story of William Davies and the 'Ringers' Feast', and to see the fine yew tree in the churchyard which is thought to be more than 1,000 years old.

Turn right, then left in 220yds (201m), following the restricted byway uphill. Cross a track and eventually bear right along the edge of Hockley Golf Course. Then, in 0.5 mile (800m), drop down through scrub to a crossing of paths. Turn left along the waymarked 'Pilgrim's Trail'.

Your long and gradual ascent of Twyford Down is rewarded by glorious vistas across rolling downland, the Itchen Valley and Winchester.

Leave the golf course at a stile, follow the path down to a gate and turn left across the motorway bridge. Go through a gate on to a path through St Catherine's Hill Nature Reserve. Descend through the valley and leave the reserve via gates. Turn right up the stepped path if you want to climb the hill. Otherwise, turn right along the path parallel with the disused Itchen Navigation to a car park. Pick up Walk 18 at Point 6.

WALK 20

# Titchfield's Historic Canal

*Explore a disused canal, a superb wetland nature reserve and a scenic clifftop path along an unspoilt stretch of Hampshire's coast.*

**DISTANCE** *6 miles (9.7km)* **MINIMUM TIME** *3hrs*
**ASCENT/GRADIENT** *114ft (35m)* ▲▲▲ **LEVEL OF DIFFICULTY** +++
**PATHS** *Canal tow path, clifftop path, tracks and field paths*
**LANDSCAPE** *Nature reserve water-meadows, coastline, open farmland*
**SUGGESTED MAP** *OS Explorer 119 Meon Valley & Portsmouth*
**START / FINISH** *Grid reference: SU 540057*
**DOG FRIENDLINESS** *Off lead by canal and along cliff top*
**PARKING** *On-street parking and car park behind community centre*
**PUBLIC TOILETS** *Titchfield and Meon Shore*

## WALK 20 DIRECTIONS

Sleepy Titchfield, with its well preserved village centre and several old pubs, lies surrounded by water-meadows and woods just a few seconds away from the busy A27 and the sprawling suburbs of Fareham. Its hard to imagine today, but Titchfield was once an important market town and a busy port in the Middle Ages due to the prosperity of its abbey, founded here in 1232, and its position beside the River Meon. By the early 17th century it was linked to the sea by a navigable channel, which allowed seagoing vessels to reach the heart of the village and trade. Whether the channel silted up or the trade decreased is not fully known but the 3rd Earl of Southampton built a dyke along the mouth of the river and in 1611 a canal was completed. Although never a success, Titchfield Canal, regarded as the second oldest artificial waterway in Britain, still exists and the tow path provides a splendid walk to the coast.

### WHILE YOU'RE THERE

Take your binoculars and visit Titchfield Haven Nature Reserve. It covers over 300 acres (121ha) of reedbed, freshwater marsh and fen from the coast to Titchfield and hides are accessible to view wintering wildfowl and waders. Permits and visitor facilities are available from Haven House along the coast road from Meon Shore. Just north of Titchfield are the impressive ruins of Titchfield Abbey, a medieval abbey that later became incorporated into a fine Tudor mansion built on the site in 1537.

From the village square walk along Church Street (beside the Co-op) to the church and bear right beside the graveyard. Cross a footbridge over the old canal and turn right along the tow path. Cross a road and keep to the tow path by the side of the canal, heading south through several gates for nearly 2 miles (3.2km). When you reach a gate, continue on towards the road to view the remnants of the sea lock.

**WHERE TO EAT AND DRINK**

There are several pubs in Titchfield for that post-walk drink or meal, notably the Bugle Hotel in The Square, the Queens Head in the High Street, and the unspoilt Wheatsheaf in East Street.

Trade is likely to have continued coming in to Titchfield from the sea as barges travelled up the canal via the sea lock, each vessel being pulled along by horses on the tow path. The canal may have declined due to the inability to maintain an opening to the sea at Meon Shore.

Just before the lane, cross the stile on the left and follow the footpath through some trees. Soon you'll reach Meon Shore and the Titchfield Haven Nature Reserve. To visit the reserve follow the footpath to the left, close to the shore road, to the visitor centre.

Building the dyke here turned the salt water estuary into a freshwater marsh and lush water-meadows, now known as Titchfield Haven. It shelters a rich variety of plants and wildlife, notably marsh marigolds, flowering rushes, wildfowl, waders and summer migrants.

When you reach a County Council sign, bear right to the road. Turn right along the road, then left beside a gate and follow the public footpath between chalets to join the Solent Way path beside a drive to Cliff Cottage. Follow the path along the top of the cliffs and enjoy the lovely views across the Solent to the Isle of Wight and Calshot Castle on the far side of Southampton Water. In 0.5 mile (800m) or so, pass in front of Sea House and descend with the path down to the beach.

Just before a freshwater inlet, follow the path inland beside a barrier. Shortly merge with the drive to Sea House and continue walking inland. At Lower Brownwich Farm, bear right along the concrete road. Ignore the footpath beside the road and keep to the drive as far as a fork. Proceed ahead (marked by a yellow arrow) and pass cottages and barns on your left, the concrete soon giving way to an earth track. Follow this track for just over 0.5 mile (800m).

Immediately before the green lane to Great Posbrook Farm, turn right through a kissing gate and follow the permissive path along the left-hand field-edge. On reaching a track turn left through a kissing gate, then right at the fork, and continue to Posbrook Lane. Turn left and keep to the lane (which can be busy) for 0.25 mile (400m) to a T-junction. Turn left, then right into St Margarets Lane and right again along West Street, following it downhill to the village square.

**WHAT TO LOOK OUT FOR**

Just before reaching Meon Shore you will pass what remains of the Earl of Southampton's sea lock built in 1611. It was part of an ambitious scheme to close the Meon estuary and replace the tidal channel with a canal. Access from the sea was by this simple lock and ships had to float in at high tides. Take a closer look at St Peter's Church in Titchfield. It may be the oldest in Hampshire and contains a fine tomb to the Earls of Southampton. The porch is said to date from the 7th century.

# Bursledon and Boatbuilding

*Exploring both sides of the yacht-filled Hamble estuary.*

**DISTANCE** *5.5 miles (8.8km)* **MINIMUM TIME** *3hrs*
**ASCENT/GRADIENT** *164ft (50m)* ▲▲▲ **LEVEL OF DIFFICULTY** +++
**PATHS** *Riverside, field and woodland paths, some stretches of road*
**LANDSCAPE** *River estuary, farmland dotted with patches of woodland*
**SUGGESTED MAP** *OS Explorer OL 22 New Forest*
**START / FINISH** *Grid reference: SU 485067*
**DOG FRIENDLINESS** *Keep dogs on lead*
**PARKING** *Pay-and-display car park by Quay in Hamble*
**PUBLIC TOILETS** *Hamble*

Hamble estuary between Bursledon and Southampton Water is one of the longest, and busiest, in Britain. The river has a long history of human activity from the first Saxon settlers, who used it as a route to the fertile areas inland, to its current status as Britain's premier yachting centre. Today, this stretch of river is filled with yachts and pleasure craft, but between the 14th and early 19th century both Hamble-le-Rice (its formal name) and Bursledon were major centres for naval shipbuilding.

The valley provided a rich supply of timber for the warships, the ironworks at nearby Hungerford Bottom supplied essential fastenings and the bend in the river at Bursledon offered the necessary shelter for the Hamble to be ideal for this vital industry. At its peak during the Napoleonic Wars the Elephant Yard, next to the Jolly Sailor pub, built the 74-gun HMS *Elephant*, Nelson's flagship at the Battle of Copenhagen. Two great local shipbuilders were George Parsons, who built the *Elephant*, and Philemon Ewer, who died in 1750 and whose epitaph states 'during the late war with France and Spain built seven large ships of war'. The best-known ship to be built at Hamble was the *Grace Dieu* for Henry V in the 15th century. It was at Hamble Common in 1545 that Henry VIII watched in horror as his flagship, the *Mary Rose*, sank with the loss of 700 men just off the coast.

The six tiny Victory Cottages you pass in Lower Swanwick, just a stone's throw from the present-day Moody's yard, were built in the late 18th century to house shipyard workers during the Napoleonic Wars. The bustling marinas and yacht moorings at Bursledon, best viewed from the terrace of the Jolly Sailor, have only appeared in the last 70 years.

Today, Hamble and Old Bursledon are a delight to explore. Hamble has a twisting main street, lined with pretty Georgian buildings, leading down to the Quay with lovely river views. Old Bursledon has a High Street but no shops, just peaceful lanes dotted with interesting buildings, in particular the timber-framed Dolphin, a former pub. Tucked away on the slopes above the river and scattered along lanes leading nowhere, you'll find it a pleasure to stroll through, especially if you pause at the Hacketts Marsh viewpoint where a well-placed bench affords the chance to admire the view.

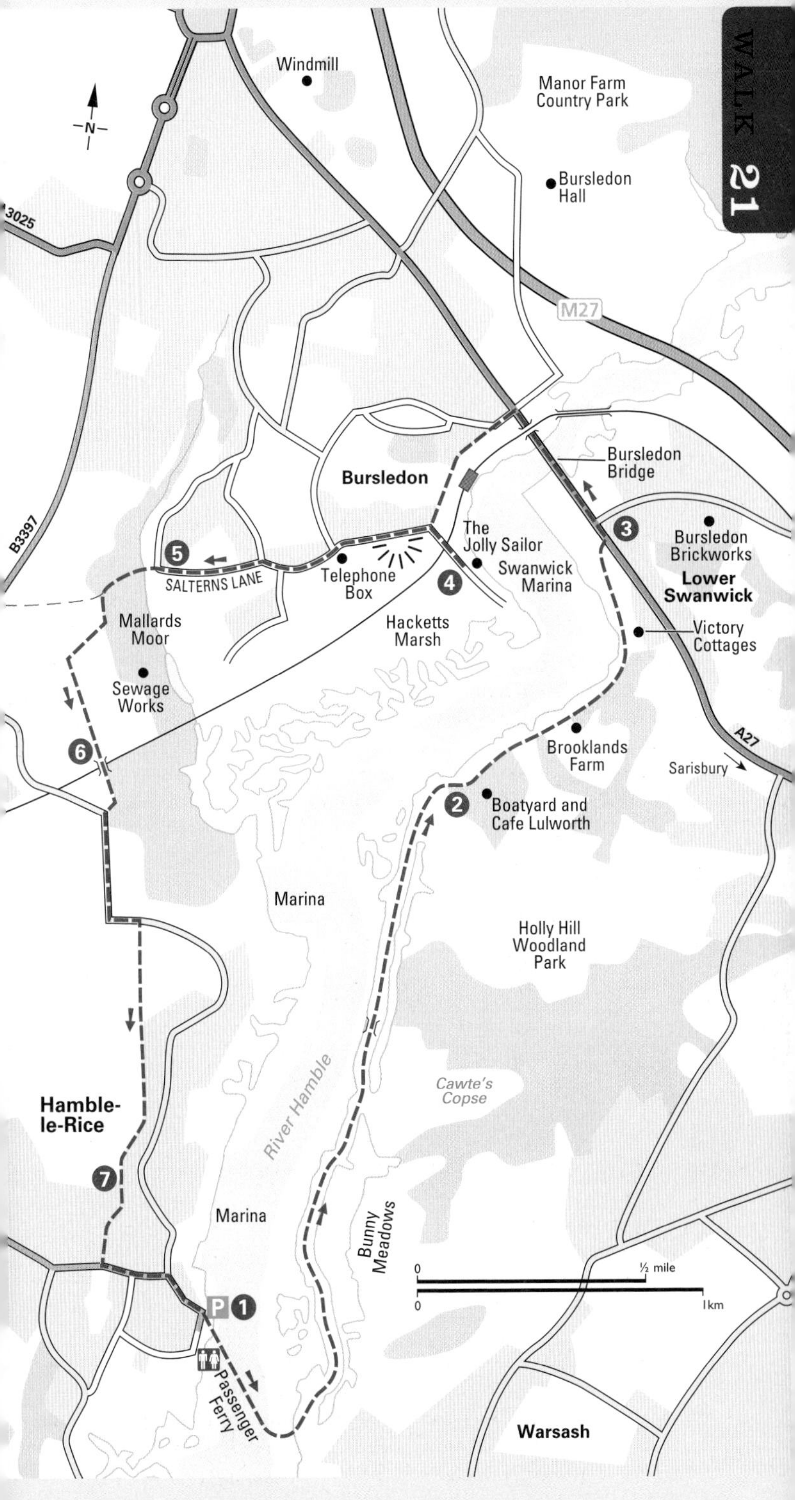


Overleaf: Old Bursledon (Walk 21)

JOLLY SAILOR

PETERHEAD

## WALK 21 DIRECTIONS

1 From the quayside car park, walk to the pontoon and take the passenger ferry across the estuary to Warsash (weather permitting; for details, visit www.hamble-warsashferry.co.uk). Turn left along the raised gravel path beside the estuary and mudflats. Cross a footbridge and continue to a gravelled parking area. During exceptionally high tides the path may flood, so walk through the car park and rejoin it by the marina.

**WHAT TO LOOK OUT FOR**

Just before high tide you may see up to 12 species of waders, including dunlin, redshank, lapwing and curlew, and wildfowl – shelduck, teal and brent geese (in winter) – feeding on the mudflats.

2 Follow the path through a boatyard, pass in front of Cafe Lulworth, and rejoin the riverside path. Keep ahead at a lane, pass Victory Cottages on your right, and continue to the A27.

3 Turn left, pass Swanwick Marina, and cross Bursledon Bridge. (Turn right before the bridge to visit Bursledon Brickworks.) Pass under the railway, turn left into Church Lane, then fork left. Turn left into Station Road. Turn left into the station car park, following signs for the Jolly Sailor. Climb a steep path to the road. Turn left at the junction, then left again to the pub.

**WHILE YOU'RE THERE**

Visit Bursledon Brickworks. Restored by a trust in 1990, it is the last surviving example of a steam-driven brickworks in the country, with a working steam engine, exhibition on the history and development of brickmaking, hands-on activities and events.

**WHERE TO EAT AND DRINK**

There's a range of pubs and tea rooms in Hamble, notably the Galley Cafe and Marco's Tea Rooms and the Bugle. Stop off at the Jolly Sailor in Bursledon for good ale or the Vine in Old Bursledon.

4 Return along the lane and fork left along the High Street into Old Bursledon. Pause at the viewpoint at Hacketts Marsh, then bear left at the telephone box along the High Street. Pass the Vine Inn and Salterns Lane, then at a right bend, bear off left by Thatched Cottage along a footpath.

5 Join a metalled lane beside the drive to the Coach House then, as the lane curves right, keep ahead beside a house called Woodlands, following the bridleway downhill to a stream. Proceed uphill through woodland (Mallards Moor). At a junction of paths on the woodland fringe, bear left with the bridleway, then at a concrete road bear right, then left to join a fenced bridleway.

6 Cross a railway bridge and soon pass a barrier to a road. Keep left round a sharp left-hand bend. Look out for a waymarked footpath on your right and follow this path behind houses for 0.5mile (800m).

7 Join a metalled path and keep ahead past modern housing to a road. Follow this out to Hamble Lane and turn left to join the High Street. At the roundabout, bear right down Lower High Street back to the Quay and car park.

# Romsey's Grand Abbey

*Explore Hampshire's best-preserved market town and the Test Valley.*

**DISTANCE** *5.75 miles (9.2km)* **MINIMUM TIME** *3hrs*

**ASCENT/GRADIENT** *120ft (36.5m)* ▲▲▲ **LEVEL OF DIFFICULTY** +++

**PATHS** *Tow path, field and woodland paths, some roads, 7 stiles*

**LANDSCAPE** *Initially urban, followed by water-meadows, rolling farmland and dense woodland*

**SUGGESTED MAP** *OS Explorer 131 Romsey, Andover & Test Valley*

**START / FINISH** *Grid reference: SU 099666*

**DOG FRIENDLINESS** *To be kept under control at all times*

**PARKING** *Romsey town centre, several pay-and-display car parks*

**PUBLIC TOILETS** *Romsey War Memorial Park*

Romsey is the best preserved of all Hampshire's market towns. Idyllically located beside the beautiful River Test, it developed around a Benedictine nunnery founded in AD 907 by Edward the Elder, son of Alfred the Great, whose daughter, Aelfreda, became the first abbess. By the end of the 10th century, there was a small town outside the perimeter walls of the abbey, whose inhabitants served the needs of the growing community of nuns. Much of the great abbey church you see today was built between 1120 and 1130 by Henry de Blois, Bishop of Winchester, but traces of the earlier Saxon church can be seen, notably two beautifully carved rood sculptures dating from AD 1000. The Abbey is now recognised as one of Europe's most impressive Norman churches, and certainly the finest in Hampshire.

## Sale of the 16th Century

Fortunately for today's visitors and for the people of the town, the magnificent abbey was saved from destruction at the Dissolution, although the surrounding convent buildings were not so lucky. In 1544 the town secured an agreement with Henry VIII and bought the Abbey and its surrounding land for £100. You can see a copy of the Bill of Sale, signed and sealed by Henry VIII in the south choir aisle. How the money was raised is still one of Romsey's great mysteries as no records have been found. A stroll around the majestic and lofty interior will reveal many of the abbey's treasures. You can marvel at the scale and splendour of the architecture, notably the massive pillars and rounded arches, view medieval paintings and tapestries, and seek out the monuments to Lord Palmerston, a Conservative Prime Minister during Queen Victoria's reign, Sir William Petty, economist and founder of the Royal Society, and Earl Mountbatten, Romsey's most famous former inhabitant.

The attractive townscape of Romsey is often eclipsed by its famous neighbour Broadlands, better known as the home of Earl Mountbatten. But against the backdrop of the abbey you will find splendid Georgian houses tucked away on winding side streets reflecting Romsey's days as a thriving brewing and market town. Opposite the Abbey stands King John's House, a hall house of 1240 and one of England's oldest surviving dwellings. The walk leaves town by the only surviving stretch of the Andover and Redbridge Canal. Completed in 1794, it was 22 miles (35.4km) long and rose 164ft (50m) via 24 locks. It was never a real success and the arrival of the railway forced its closure in 1857. The tow path takes you into the Test Valley and you will soon be walking beside the crystal clear waters of Hampshire's most famous chalk stream. Beyond the Duke's Head, a gentle climb through Squabb Wood leads you back to the water-meadows close to the Test. As you head towards Saddler's Mill, the view across the river to the Abbey rising above town is delightful.

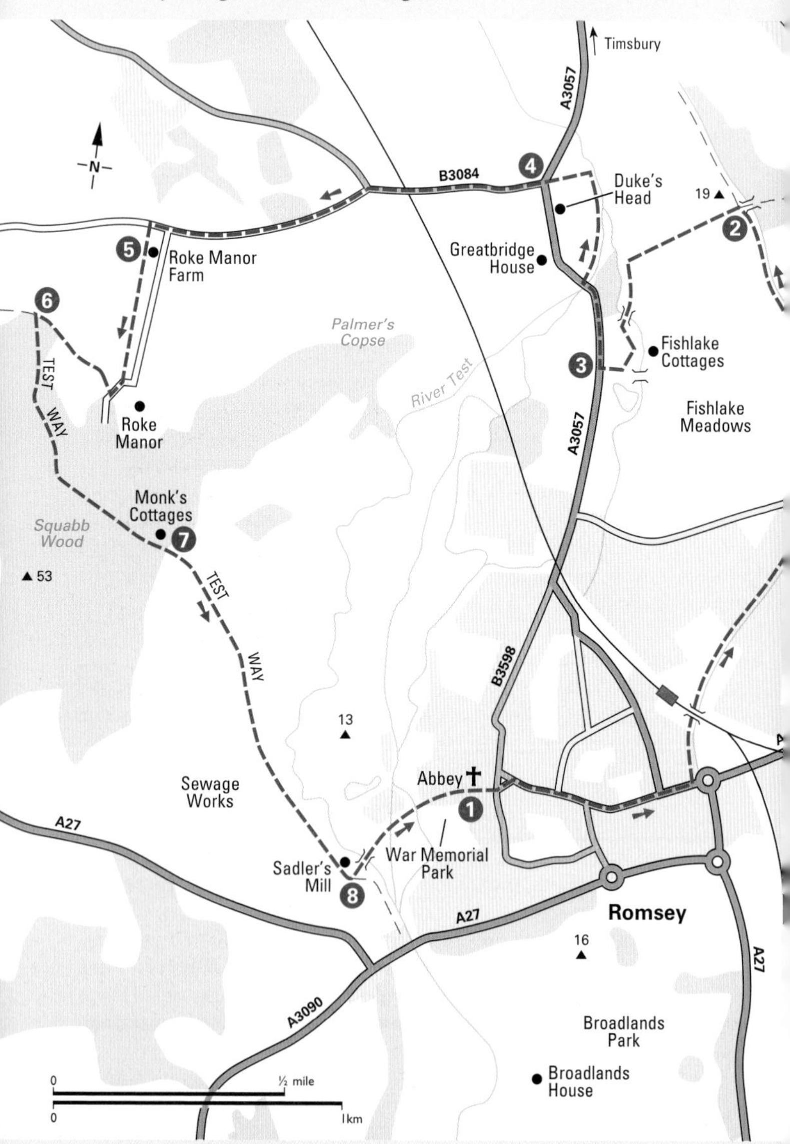

## WALK 22 DIRECTIONS

1 From the Market Square head east along the Hundred and continue into Winchester Road. At the roundabout, turn left up steps to join a footpath to Timsbury. Walk alongside the old canal as it passes under the railway and then a road bridge, and leave town into open meadowland.

2 At a crossing of paths (with a bridge right), turn left and then walk across the meadows. Bear right across bridges, and follow the path to reach the River Test. Turn left along the river bank, cross a wooden bridge and walk alongside the opposite bank to a stile and track by a bridge and house. Turn right to the A3057 and turn right.

3 Follow the pavement and cross the River Test, then take the footpath immediately right alongside the river. Pass a bridge, then follow the official diversion left around a house to a track. Turn left to the main road and the Duke's Head on the left.

4 Cross the road to join the B3084, signed to Roke Manor. Carefully walk along this busy road (some verges) for 0.5 mile (800m), then just beyond the railway bridge, fork left for Roke Manor. Pass the Manor's entrance and take the drive on the left.

5 Pass Roke Manor Farm, then on nearing the Manor, bear half right along the road for 60yds (55m). Take the footpath right (can be overgrown) and shortly bear right through a hedge, then left around a field. Skirt the copse on your left to locate a Test Way sign and turn left through a gate.

**WHERE TO EAT AND DRINK**

There are plenty of pubs, restaurants and cafés in Romsey, notably Miss Moody's Tudor Tea Room; the Olive Tree; the Courtyard Coffee House; the Three Tuns and the Duke's Head.

6 Walk into Squabb Wood on a bracken-lined path, cross two plank bridges to a junction of paths. Keep left with the Test Way and go through the wood, via plank bridges and stiles, looking out for the Test Way markers.

**WHILE YOU'RE THERE**

Visit Broadlands, the home of Lord Mountbatten. This elegant Palladian mansion enjoys a lovely setting by the River Test and you can view inside the house.

7 Leave the wood and bear half right across the field to stiles and a footbridge, then bear slightly left to further stiles and a footbridge. Keep to the left-hand edge of the field, pass through two kissing gates and follow the track as it bears left between houses to the River Test by Sadler's Mill.

8 Bear left by the mill and leave the Test Way. Cross the river, follow a tarmac path and soon pass the War Memorial Park. Continue along a road close to the abbey back into the Market Square.

**WHAT TO LOOK OUT FOR**

If visiting King John's House (off Church Street), look for the small exposed section of knuckle bone floor, made from cattle bones in the 17th century, and the graffiti scratched by daggers on the plaster walls in 1306. In the autumn, at Saddlers Mill on the Test, look out for salmon leaping the weir as they return to their spawning grounds.

# King's Somborne – A Palace by the Test

*Enjoy the Test Valley and the fine downland scenery around King's Somborne, once the haunt of Norman kings.*

**DISTANCE** *3 miles (4.8km)* **MINIMUM TIME** *1hr 30min*

**ASCENT/GRADIENT** *138ft (42m)* ▲▲▲ **LEVEL OF DIFFICULTY** +++

**PATHS** *Former railway track, field paths, tracks and road, 1 stile*

**LANDSCAPE** *River valley, open farmland and downland*

**SUGGESTED MAP** *OS Explorer 131 Romsey, Andover & Test Valley*

**START / FINISH** *Grid reference: SU 345305*

**DOG FRIENDLINESS** *Off lead along the Test Way, otherwise keep under control*

**PARKING** *Test Way car park at Horsebridge, opposite John of Gaunt pub*

**PUBLIC TOILETS** *None en route*

The tiny hamlet of Horsebridge is situated beside the River Test at the exact point where the original Roman road from Winchester to Old Sarum crossed the river. It is believed the Normans revived the old road to provide easy access from a hunting lodge, at Clarendon in Wiltshire, to a palace that probably existed at King's Somborne, and the huge deer park that occupied land between the village and the Test. The close proximity of the former deer park to Horsebridge is remembered in the name of the pub, the John of Gaunt, who acquired the hunting ground after his marriage to Blanche of Lancaster in 1359.

## Hollows and Bumps

King's Somborne takes its name from where the 'som' (swine) drank at or crossed the 'borne' (stream), with the royal connection dating back at least to Saxon times. In the Domesday Survey of 1086 the manor was held by the Crown. Tradition has it that John of Gaunt (1340–99), the English prince, fourth son of Edward III and father of Henry IV, had his palace behind the church in King's Somborne. Various hollows and humps can be seen as you cross the field, indicating the remains of a building, but excavations have only revealed evidence of an Anglo-Saxon settlement. It is known that a large manor house existed here in 1591. The term 'John of Gaunt's Palace' is a more recent connotation based on the fact that the manor of King's Somborne was inherited by his wife in 1362. The Deer Park was created by William Briwere before 1200 and you can see parts of the 14th-century enclosing banks and yew trees as you leave the Test Valley and begin ascending on the Clarendon Way, and banks up to 10ft (3m) can be seen alongside the Horsebridge road.

As you stroll through the village you should also spy the village school, situated next to the church. It was founded in 1842 by Revd Richard Dawes and built from knapped flints salvaged from the nearby ruins of the manor house. Dawes was an educational innovator and his progressive teaching methods attracted great interest. Prime Minister, Lord Russell and Florence Nightingale were among the early visitors. According to Dawes, its construction was inspired by the need to raise moral standards of those who lived here, as he found the parish run down and demoralised when he moved to the village in 1837.

Your route through the attractive Test Valley follows the disused Test Valley Railway, or the 'Sprat and Winkle line' as it was affectionately known. The line was built in 1865, replacing the canal that ran between Redbridge and Andover, but closed during the Beeching era in 1964. The Test Way, a long distance path that traverses Hampshire from Inkpen Beacon in the north to Totton in the south, follows it for 10 miles (16.1km) from Lower Brook to Fullerton.

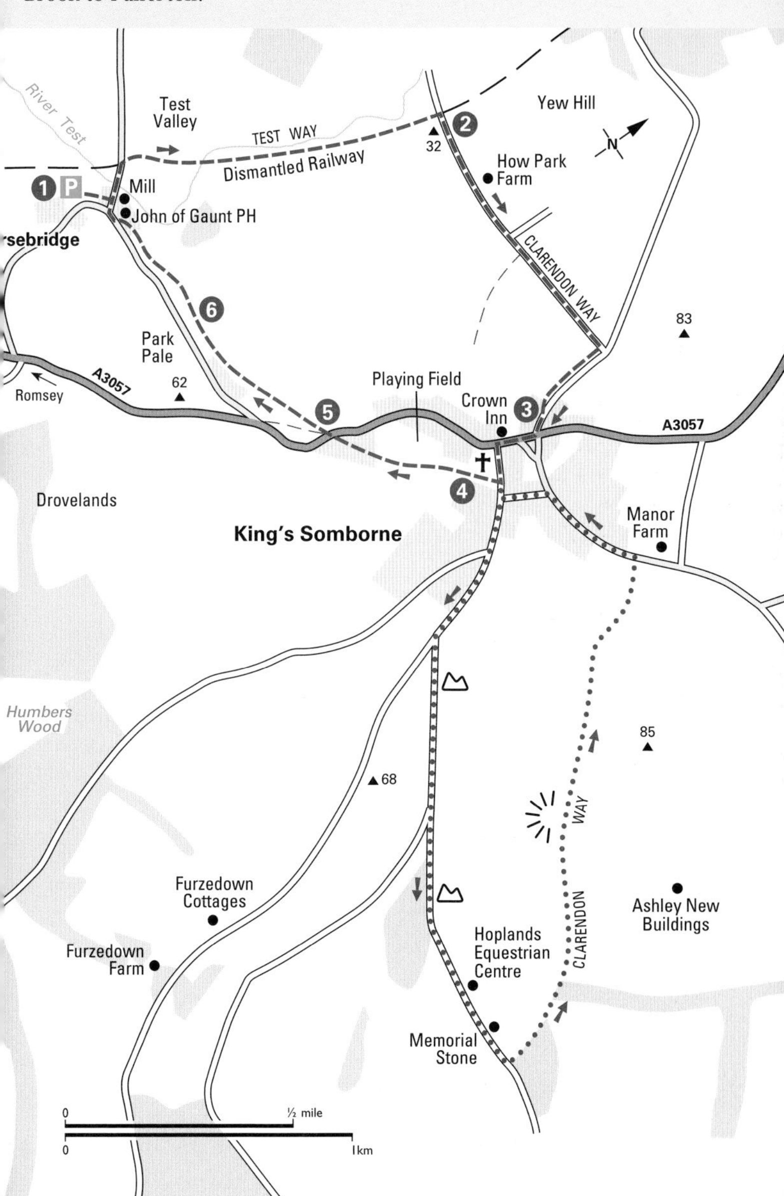

## WALK 23 DIRECTIONS

1 Leave the car park and turn left, opposite the John of Gaunt. Cross the River Test and turn right along the Test Way, dropping down on to the old railway line. In 0.75 mile (1.2km), pass beside a gate and turn right along the Clarendon Way.

2 Climb out of the valley, the track becoming metalled at the top. Ignore turnings left and right, keeping straight ahead until, just before a T-junction, you turn right with a waymarker down the left-hand edge of a field towards King's Somborne.

### WHERE TO EAT AND DRINK

The thatched Crown Inn in King's Somborne offers a homely atmosphere and good bar meals. Expect a warm welcome and wholesome, home-made food at the John of Gaunt, close to the Test Way at Horsebridge and popular with walkers.

3 Turn right along the lane, then right again at the A3057 into the village. Turn left along Church Road opposite the Crown Inn. Just beyond the churchyard wall, take the narrow footpath right alongside the churchyard.

### WHILE YOU'RE THERE

Instead of turning right along the Test Way from Horsebridge, turn left and follow it for 150yds (137m) to pass Horsebridge Station. Although private, you can glimpse this beautifully preserved station, complete with waiting room, parcel office, signal box, platform and an L&SWR third-class carriage. The atmosphere of bygone steam days can be relived in this nostalgic scene.

### WHAT TO LOOK OUT FOR

In the striking Church of St Peter and St Paul in King's Somborne you can see one of Hampshire's oldest monuments, that of a priest, William Bristowe who was vicar here between 1305 and 1327. On the chancel floor you should note two of England's oldest brasses, dated around 1380, which are thought to be of two of John of Gaunt's stewards. The war memorial in front of the church was designed by the famous architect Edwin Lutyens, who also designed Marsh Court, an elegant mansion overlooking the Test Valley near Stockbridge.

4 Go through a gate and enter rough grassland. This is where John of Gaunt's palace is supposed to have existed. Cross to a further gate and enter a playing field. Bear diagonally left across the field to the top left-hand corner and join a grassy path leading to a close of houses. Turn right then, in a few paces, bear off left along a narrow fenced path between properties to the main road.

5 Cross straight over and go through a gate into pasture. Take the footpath half right across the field to its boundary. Keep to the path that leads you through gardens, via small gates, to a field.

6 Continue ahead towards a house and shortly cross the drive in front of it. Maintain direction through further pasture to reach a stile and lane in Horsebridge. Turn right, then right again at the junction and turn left back into the Test Way car park.

# King's Somborne and the Clarendon Way

*A longer loop takes you above the Test Valley to a sad reminder of wartime, then on to the Clarendon Way.*

**See map and information panel for Walk 23**



DISTANCE *6 miles (9.7km)* MINIMUM TIME *3hrs*

ASCENT/GRADIENT *347ft (106m)* ▲▲▲ LEVEL OF DIFFICULTY +++

## WALK 24 DIRECTIONS (Walk 23 option)

Instead of taking the footpath right beside the churchyard in King's Somborne, after Point ❸, keep ahead along the lane. Ignore lanes left and right and gradually climb away from the village. At the top of the hill, turn left at the fork and follow a metalled drive. Disregard the right of way to the right and gently climb beside paddocks, following the drive past Hoplands Equestrian Centre. Keep ahead along a track and shortly pass a memorial stone on your left.

This simple stone commemorates four unknown German airmen who were killed above Ashley Down when their Junkers JU88 was shot down by a Spitfire in August 1940. It was Squadron Leader Bob Doe who was scrambled from Middle Wallop to intercept the JU88 as it returned from a bombing raid on Manchester. After only seven days in action, he had already shot down four planes and this, his fifth, would make him an 'ace'. Having riddled the plane with bullets and watched it crash in a field near King's Somborne, he thought it would be satisfying to see the wreckage of the plane. On seeing the German airmen shot to pieces he was sickened by the consequences of his triumph and what felt like a victory now seemed more like a kind of execution. He vowed he would never sightsee again.

Continue along the track and shortly turn left along the Clarendon Way through a copse to a gate. Bear right and walk downhill beside paddocks, with splendid views across the Test Valley. Cross a stile in the field corner and walk an enclosed path; then, follow the right-hand edge of fields before descending to a lane in King's Somborne.

The Clarendon Way is a 26 mile (41.8km) long distance path linking Winchester with Salisbury and is named after a hunting lodge for Norman kings in Wiltshire.

Turn left and walk through the village, following the lane left to a T-junction. Turn right and then left along the footpath beside the churchyard wall to rejoin Walk 23 at Point ❹.

# Meandering around Mottisfont

*Combine glorious woodland and riverside walking, along the River Dun, with a visit to a 12th-century Augustinian priory.*

**DISTANCE** *3.5 miles (5.7km)* **MINIMUM TIME** *1hr 45min*

**ASCENT/GRADIENT** *164ft (50m)* ▲▲▲ **LEVEL OF DIFFICULTY** +++

**PATHS** *Easy woodland trails and field paths, 2 stiles*

**LANDSCAPE** *Water-meadows, farmland and National Trust woodland*

**SUGGESTED MAP** *OS Explorer 131 Romsey, Andover & Test Valley*

**START / FINISH** *Grid reference: SU 315277*

**DOG FRIENDLINESS** *Can be let off lead in Spearywell Wood*

**PARKING** *National Trust car park at Spearywell Wood*

**PUBLIC TOILETS** *In abbey gardens (only if visiting Abbey)*

## WALK 25 DIRECTIONS

This short walk explores the National Trust estate at Mottisfont. Set picturesquely beside the River Test and around the walls of a former 12th-century priory, Mottisfont is a charming village of thatched cottages and Georgian houses, complete with a splendid listed church and an old tithe barn. The village name is derived from 'moot's font' or 'spring of the meeting place', which rises in a deep pool in the abbey grounds.

Whether you start the walk from Mottisfont Abbey car park (seasonal opening) or from Spearywell Wood, you will find strolling through the village a real delight. Beginning from the latter, the walk explores good estate paths through woodland, then gradually descends into the Dun Valley, offering you serene views west across rolling downland into fertile Wiltshire.

### WHILE YOU'RE THERE

If you're here in June, make sure you see the National Collection of Old Fashioned Roses, in the walled kitchen garden of the abbey in 1972. The colour and heady perfume of thousands of roses on a balmy June evening is a magical experience.

Pass beside the barrier opposite the Spearywell Wood car park entrance to join a woodland path. Ignore paths left and right and pass through a tall conifer plantation; then, where the path reaches a junction, turn left (by a concrete marker stone). Bear right with the estate path at the next junction, then at the staggered junction (by a short cut sign to the abbey), bear left, then immediately right through woodland. Descend through the woodland fringe to a junction and turn left across a field. At a barrier and crossing of paths, zig-zag right, then left, following an estate path along the woodland edge. Continue beside fencing, eventually passing beneath the railway to a footbridge over the River Dun.

The swiftly flowing River Dun, a tributary of the Test, was also known as the Barge River. At one time there were plans to develop a canal to link Southampton and Salisbury, but the scheme was never completed.

Don't cross the river. Turn left through the kissing gate and follow the path across meadow and rough, marshy pasture, crossing two plank bridges to a double stile at the end by the oak trees. Bear right through a gate, and follow the fence on your left. Continue through a copse, passing a spring, then an isolated thatched cottage to a stile by a gate. Proceed along the left-hand field-edge and follow the grassy track to the railway. Cross the line (take great care – look and listen), then follow the track to a stile and the B3084. Turn right to visit the Mill Arms at Dunbridge. Cross over to join a field path which soon bears left to reach a lane. Turn right and enter Mottisfont.

Originally an Augustinian priory church, founded by William Briwere in 1201, Mottisfont Abbey never achieved the full status of an abbey and struggled to survive until the Dissolution of the Monasteries. Between 1536 and 1540 it was acquired by William, Lord Sandys who converted the buildings into a mansion. It was during the 18th century that much of the medieval cloisters were destroyed and the romantic title 'abbey' given to the building. Although mainly private, you can still see some medieval arches, the 13th-century monks' cellarium and a masterpiece of trompe-l'oeil work by Rex Whistler, one of the great British artists of the 20th century, in the Drawing Room. You will find the sweeping lawns and mature trees which run down to the River Test very peaceful and well worth spending a few quiet moments in.

### WHAT TO LOOK OUT FOR

You should not miss St Andrew's Church in Mottisfont. Dating from the 12th century and Grade I listed, it contains more 15th-century stained glass that any other Hampshire church, a fine Norman chancel and a rare clock mechanism c1620, the only other one in working order is in Salisbury Cathedral. While strolling the magnificent grounds surrounding Mottisfont Abbey, look out for the old Ice House behind the stables. Few remain in the county in such good condition.

At the T-junction, turn right for the entrance to Mottisfont Abbey. Retrace your steps along the road and bear right to a junction, opposite the abbey gates. Turn left along Bengers Lane and take the path right, diagonally across the field towards a lone oak tree. Cross a plank bridge and proceed through the next field to a gate. Turn right along the road for 150yds (137m) for the car park.

### WHERE TO EAT AND DRINK

The Abbey has its own licensed restaurant. A short diversion just beyond half way will lead you to the Mill Arms at Dunbridge for well-presented food, decent ales and a pleasant summer garden.

# A Testing Trail from Stockbridge

*Tales of fish, fillies and forts accompany you on this downland walk to Danebury Ring from the River Test's fishing capital.*

**DISTANCE** *7 miles (11.3km)* **MINIMUM TIME** *3hrs 30min*

**ASCENT/GRADIENT** *492ft (150m)* ▲▲▲ **LEVEL OF DIFFICULTY** +++

**PATHS** *Wide byways, field paths and railway track, 3 stiles*

**LANDSCAPE** *Open downland and river valley*

**SUGGESTED MAP** *OS Explorer 131 Romsey, Andover & Test Valley*

**START / FINISH** *Grid reference: SU 355351*

**DOG FRIENDLINESS** *Can run free on Danebury Hill (prohibited in hill-fort area)*

**PARKING** *Along Stockbridge High Street*

**PUBLIC TOILETS** *Danebury Hill (April to October) and Stockbridge*

Stockbridge has developed from a frontier stronghold, built across the Test Valley by the Saxons to defend Wessex from marauding Danes, and a prosperous market town attracting Welsh sheep drovers en route to the markets in Surrey and Kent, to become Hampshire's 'fishing capital'.

The clean waters of the River Test – one of England's finest chalk streams – are renowned for their trout fishing. On your journey down the long main street you will cross at least six branches of the Test and a short diversion on to Common Marsh will give you rare access to the river bank. Much of the river bank in this area is reserved exclusively for wealthy fishing syndicates. The imposing 17th-century Grosvenor Hotel is the headquarters of the oldest and most select fishing club in the world, the Houghton Club, founded in 1822. Membership is limited to 24 and the club rigorously controls the fishing of the Test. The room above the distinctive overhanging porch, built so that coach travellers could alight under cover, is where the club's records have been kept since the club began.

## Danish Dock

Towards the end of your walk, as you cross the valley at Longstock, you will see one of the distinctive, thatched fishing huts that are dotted along the banks of the river. Beside the hut, on a bridge across the river, you will notice some iron traps. Originally made from hazel they were lowered into the river to catch eels. Behind the hut and hidden in the reeds, are the remains of a 'Danish Dock', built to harbour flat-bottomed longboats. These may well have belonged to King Canute, who is known to have sailed up the Test and destroyed Romsey.

Before fishing for sport dominated village life, Stockbridge maintained its importance and wealth by becoming a famous horse racing centre during the 19th century. Between 1753 and 1898 a racecourse existed high on the downs above the village and was a venue for important meetings in the racing calendar, on a par with Ascot and Goodwood. A frequent visitor was the Prince of Wales (later Edward VIII), who rented two properties in the village, one for himself and the other for Lillie Langtry. At its peak the area had nine racing stables. You can still see the old, ivy-covered stadium across the field below Chattis Hill as you make your way towards Danebury Hill.

Your long and gradual climb out of the Test Valley culminates at an important Iron Age hill-fort on top of Danebury Hill. The ancient earthwork covers an area of 13 acres (7.3ha) and is a magnificent sight, with a double bank and ditch and an inner rampart up to 16ft (5m) high. It was occupied by the Atrebates, a Celtic people, from about 550 to 100 BC and excavations have revealed a detailed picture of Iron Age society. Discoveries include a pattern of streets, circular houses, shrines and storage pits, and over 100,000 pieces of pottery. You can see many of the best finds in the Iron Age Museum in Andover. Equally rewarding are the far-reaching views across Hampshire and into Wiltshire from its summit, a vista that can take in six other hill-forts on a clear day.

## WALK 26 DIRECTIONS

**1** Walk west along the main street (A30), crossing the numerous braided streams of the River Test. Begin the climb out of the village and, just after the start of the dual carriageway, bear off to the left along Roman Road. Keep ahead at the end of the road, walking along the narrow defined path that climbs Meon Hill.

❷ Just before Houghton Down Farm on your left, look out for a stile in the hedge on your right. Cross this and walk along the right-hand edge of a small orchard to a stile. Cross the A30 (take care), then walk through the gap opposite and along the right-hand edge of a large field.

**WHERE TO EAT AND DRINK**

There's a good range of pubs in Stockbridge, notably the White Hart and the Greyhound. Afternoon tea is served at the Grosvenor Hotel. Imaginative pub food can be enjoyed at the Peat Spade in Longstock (open all day, with food at lunchtimes and evenings).

❸ Ignore the footpath turning on the right and keep to the main path, eventually bearing left with the field-edge to a grassy track leading to a gate and stile. Turn immediately right along a wide, hedged track and follow this for 0.75 mile (1.2km) to a junction. To visit Danebury Hill Fort, turn left towards The Wallops for 400yds (366m), then left again along the drive to the car park and access to Danebury Hill.

**WHILE YOU'RE THERE**

Take the path by the side of Lillies tea room to access the 200 acres (81ha) known as Common Marsh. It was granted to the lords of the manor by charter some 900 years ago, allowing residents of Stockbridge to use it to graze their cattle – up to six beasts each. Now owned by the National Trust, it is one of the few places along the length of the Test that you can actually walk on the bank of the trout-filled river. Just to the south of Stockbridge you'll find Houghton Lodge Gardens overlooking the tranquil beauty of the River Test. Spacious lawns with fine trees surround the 18th-century fishing lodge and sweep down to the river.

**WHAT TO LOOK OUT FOR**

A short distance along the Houghton road is the thatched Drovers' House. Dating from the 12th century, it was formerly an inn and provided lodgings for sheep drovers on their way from Wales to fairs in the South East The inscription in Welsh reads 'seasoned hay, delicious pastures, good beer, comfortable beds'.

❹ Retrace your steps back to the road junction you passed before Danebury Hill and take the byway to the left beneath a height barrier. Remain on this track as it descends back into the Test Valley. Eventually it becomes metalled as it enters the village of Longstock.

❺ At the T-junction by the church turn left, then right beside the Peat Spade pub, along 'The Bunny'. Cross numerous streams that make up the River Test, notably one with a thatched fishing hut and replica metal eel traps.

❻ Just before crossing a bridge over the disused Test Valley railway, and the A3057, take the narrow footpath on the right. Drop down and turn right along the old railway trackbed (here forming a part of the Test Way) for about a mile (1.6km) to the A3057. Taking great care, turn right, walking along the roadside for 100yds (91m) to the roundabout, then follow the grassy verge to the next roundabout by the White Hart Inn. Turn right here to return to Stockbridge and your car.

# Murder in Harewood Forest



*In search of Deadman's Plack Monument and grim legends of murder.*

**DISTANCE** *7.5 miles (12.1km)* **MINIMUM TIME** *4hrs*
**ASCENT/GRADIENT** *295ft (90m)* ▲▲▲ **LEVEL OF DIFFICULTY** +++
**PATHS** *Field, woodland paths and tracks, 3 stiles*
**LANDSCAPE** *Water-meadow, rolling farmland and thick woodland*
**SUGGESTED MAP** *OS Explorer 144 Basingstoke, Alton & Whitchurch*
**START / FINISH** *Grid reference: SU 426439*
**DOG FRIENDLINESS** *Can run free through Harewood Forest*
**PARKING** *Car park at St Nicholas Church or by village hall*
**PUBLIC TOILETS** *None en route*

Hidden away in the heart of Harewwood Forest, at an eerie place called Deadman's Plack, is a sinister grey monument. Despite standing over 70ft (20m) tall, it's shrouded by trees and can be difficult to find. The reasons for its construction will send shivers down your spine.

Colonel Iremonger, owner of Wherwell Priory, erected the monument in 1825 to commemorate the spot where Edgar, grandson of Alfred the Great and King of England is supposed to have murdered his friend Athelwold in AD 963. The events leading to this bloody deed make a classic tale of love, jealousy and hate. Eager to marry again following the death of his first wife, Edgar sent one of his trusted courtiers, Earl Athelwold, to visit Elfrida, daughter of Ordgar, Earl of Devon and a renowned beauty, to see if the reports of her beauty were true. But Althelwold fell in love with her and, before wooing and marrying her, sent back a message that she was ugly and would be unsuitable as a queen. Edgar soon found out he had been deceived and Elfrida, having realised that she had lost her chance at becoming queen, turned her charms towards Edgar. The King too was smitten and fell in love. He could not forgive Athelwold and it is said that Edgar and Elfrida plotted together to murder him.

Edgar invited the Earl on a hunting trip in Harewood Forest and at Deadman's Plack stabbed him to death. He promptly married Elfrida and they had a son, Ethelred. Following the King's death in AD 975, his son Edward from his first marriage succeeded him to the throne. Jealous of her stepson and anxious for her own son Ethelred to be king, she stabbed Edward to death at Corfe Castle in AD 978. Elfrida, stricken with remorse, founded a nunnery on the banks of the River Test at Wherwell, 3 miles (4.8km) south of Deadman's Plack. Haunted by her own conscience she lived a life of penitence until her death in 1002.

Leaving the Deadman's Plack Copse behind you, the walk soon merges with the Test Way. This well-waymarked trail leads you back into the Test Valley and Longparish. Stretching for 3 miles (4.8km) along the River Test, the village was originally known as Middleton before its name was superseded by its nickname 'Longparish'.

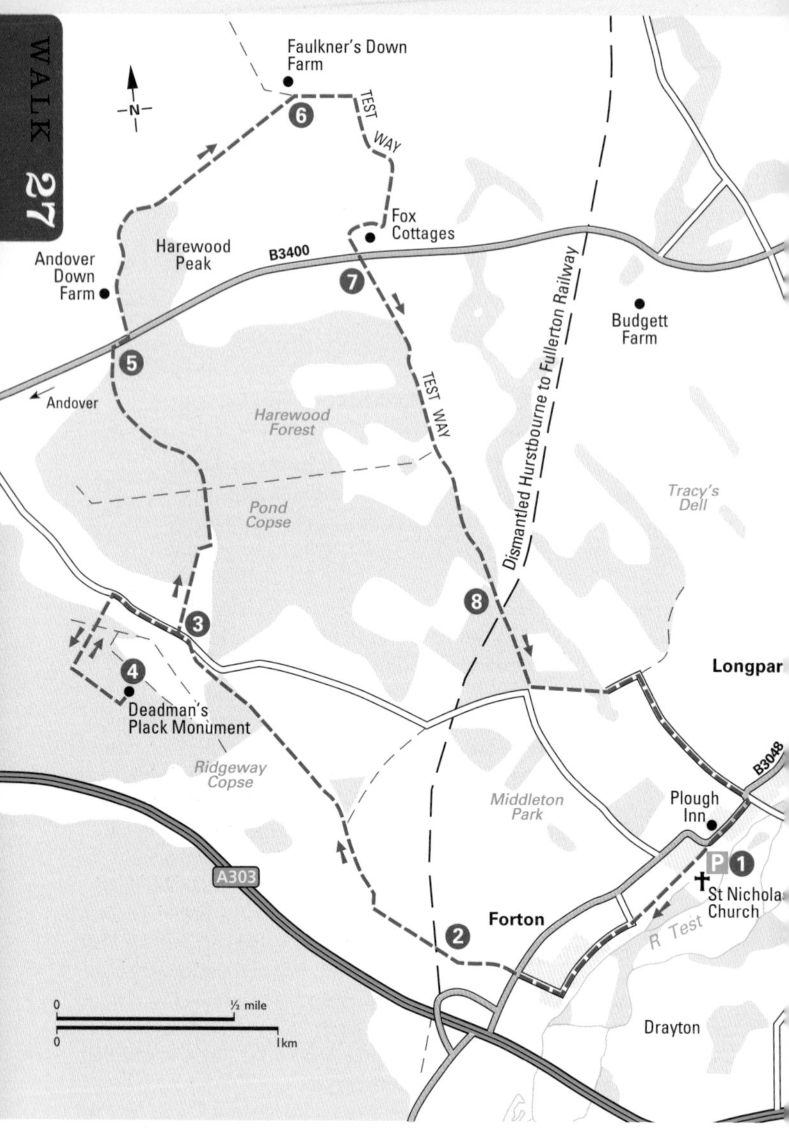


## WALK 27 DIRECTIONS

**1** Walk through the churchyard, exit via the gate and follow the Test Way across water-meadow. Go through two gates and bear left along the lane into the village of Forton. Go round the sharp right-hand bend by a barn to a T-junction. Pass through the gate opposite to a field path, then bear right along a rough track.

**2** Cross the course of the old Hurstbourne-to-Fullerton branch line, then keep ahead beside a hedge on right. Go through a gap at the top corner of the field, then bear right at a marker post, still following the hedge on right. Continue into the next field and follow the waymarked path beside a small wood on the right. Shortly, cross a track to follow the path along the left-hand edge of a large

WHILE YOU'RE THERE

Take a closer look at St Nicholas's Church. Although much restored in Victorian times, it dates from the 13th century and features a handsome, chequered stone and flint tower constructed in the 15th century.

field at the base of a shallow valley. On reaching the field corner, keep ahead through trees to a lane.

3 To visit Deadman's Plack turn left along the lane for 500yds (457m). Turn left over a stile and cross the meadow into woods. Keep ahead over a track, then drop gently to a crossways and turn left along the signed 'Permissive footpath to the monument'.

4 Retrace your steps back to point 3. Turn left then, after 50yds (46m), cross the stile in the hedge on your right and follow a path between fields and alongside woodland. Bear left by some birch trees to join the main track through Harewood Forest. Keep ahead at a crossing of paths by a large conifer tree and eventually join a gravel drive to the B3400.

WHAT TO LOOK OUT FOR

You will cross the former track of the Hurstbourne-to-Fullerton branch railway. Built in 1885, it connected with the London-to-Salisbury line and was a favourite with Queen Victoria, who asked for the Royal Trains to be routed along the line whenever she travelled to Southampton. Longparish station, now Harewood Halt and situated across the A303, was used in the original version of *The Ghost Train*, filmed in 1927. Passenger trains ceased running in 1931, although freight trains used the line until 1956, including those that carried ammunition during the Second World War to Harewood Forest where it was stored.

5 Turn right, then almost immediately left up the drive to Andover Down Farm. Keep to the right of the farm and a small industrial site. Bear off left at gates to a house and follow the track right. Head downhill towards Faulkner's Down Farm.

WHERE TO EAT AND DRINK

On completing the walk, retire to the comfortable Plough Inn for real ales and a decent menu. Expect lunchtime baguettes, open sandwiches, and home-made chutney with your ploughman's. There's a set-price Ramblers' Lunch, too.

6 At the farm, bear right along its metalled drive. Proceed downhill, turning right at the 'Private Road, No Thoroughfare' sign on to a track between fields, signed 'Test Way - TW'. Go through a gap in the hedge (TW), then follow the left-hand field-edge to a stile near cottages. Bear left on the drive to the B3400.

7 Cross the road and stile opposite and follow the grassy track (TW) beside rolling arable land. Gently climb, then descend, to join a stony track beneath the beech canopy. Shortly, bear left (TW) along a narrow path to a metalled track.

8 Turn left, cross the old railway and keep left at a fork on to a gravel track. Follow this left and shortly reach a junction of tracks. Turn right (TW) to Longparish. At the village lane, turn right, passing the Plough Inn, back to the church or village hall.

# The Hampshire Highlands

*The panoramas are breathtaking on this invigorating walk through the hidden combes and heady heights of the North Hampshire Downs.*

**DISTANCE** *5.5 miles (8.8km)* **MINIMUM TIME** *3hrs*

**ASCENT/GRADIENT** *609ft (186m)* ▲▲▲ **LEVEL OF DIFFICULTY** +++

**PATHS** *Ridge tracks, field paths and country road*

**LANDSCAPE** *Downland, hidden combes and rolling farmland*

**SUGGESTED MAP** *OS Explorers 131 Romsey, Andover & Test Valley, 144 Basingstoke, Alton & Whitchurch*

**START / FINISH** *Grid reference: SU 416575*

**DOG FRIENDLINESS** *Let them off lead along ridge-top track*

**PARKING** *Along village street by the Plough*

**PUBLIC TOILETS** *None en route*

The far north-west corner of Hampshire is dominated by a stretch of high chalk downland tumbling across the Berkshire border close to Walbury Hill, the highest chalk hill in England at 947ft (288m), commonly known as the North Hampshire Downs. This a remote and peaceful area, with an impressive chalk ridge that affords a magnificent panorama north across Newbury and Berkshire, and west into Wiltshire. South of this lofty escarpment lie rolling hills dotted with ancient woodland, hidden combes and seemingly unchanging isolated communities.

## Hill Country

Venture west away from the busy A34 and the A343 and you'll find yourself on lonely single-track roads, heading through undisturbed hill country, where glorious views unfolding to villages, such as Faccombe, Combe, Linkenholt and Vernham Dean. The area must be one of the few areas in the county that you can pause and enjoy the peace and quiet that surrounds you, without being rudely interrupted by the intruding roar of car engines. Sheep dot the pastures, in high summer the cotton reels of hay, fresh from harvesting, line the fields, and the mewing of buzzards fills the air.

## Highest Point

You begin your walk in the long straggling village of Ashmansworth, which at 770ft (235m) is the highest medieval village on chalk anywhere in England. There's a well-spaced mix of farmhouses and cottages, built of typical Hampshire flint, brick, timber and thatch. Take a stroll down to the totally unspoilt 12th-century church to view medieval wall paintings and the memorial to the composer Gerald Finzi before setting off for Pilot Hill. Reached via an ancient ridge track, formerly a sheep-droving route, Pilot Hill is, at 937ft (286m), the highest point in Hampshire. As you leave the Wayfarers Walk, pause to absorb the view across the Berkshire Vale into Oxfordshire. Just a few paces further on, you'll find the view south, across the heart of Hampshire, equally impressive.

Faccombe, the most northerly village in the county, is a classic example of an unspoilt estate village. Centred around a large Georgian manor house, it boasts a typical village pond, attractive brick-built cottages and a welcoming village inn, also estate-owned. Named after the Saxon chieftain Facca, the village was once known as Faccombe Upstreet to distinguish it from Faccombe Netherton, now simply Netherton, 1 mile (1.6km) to the west. The latter was at one time the the main centre of population, once having a 13th-century church. It is only in the last 160 years that the bulk of the population has moved up the hill to Faccombe, where the Church of St Barnabas was built in 1886 to serve the village, and where you will find the beautifully decorated Norman font and several 17th-century memorials from the original church.

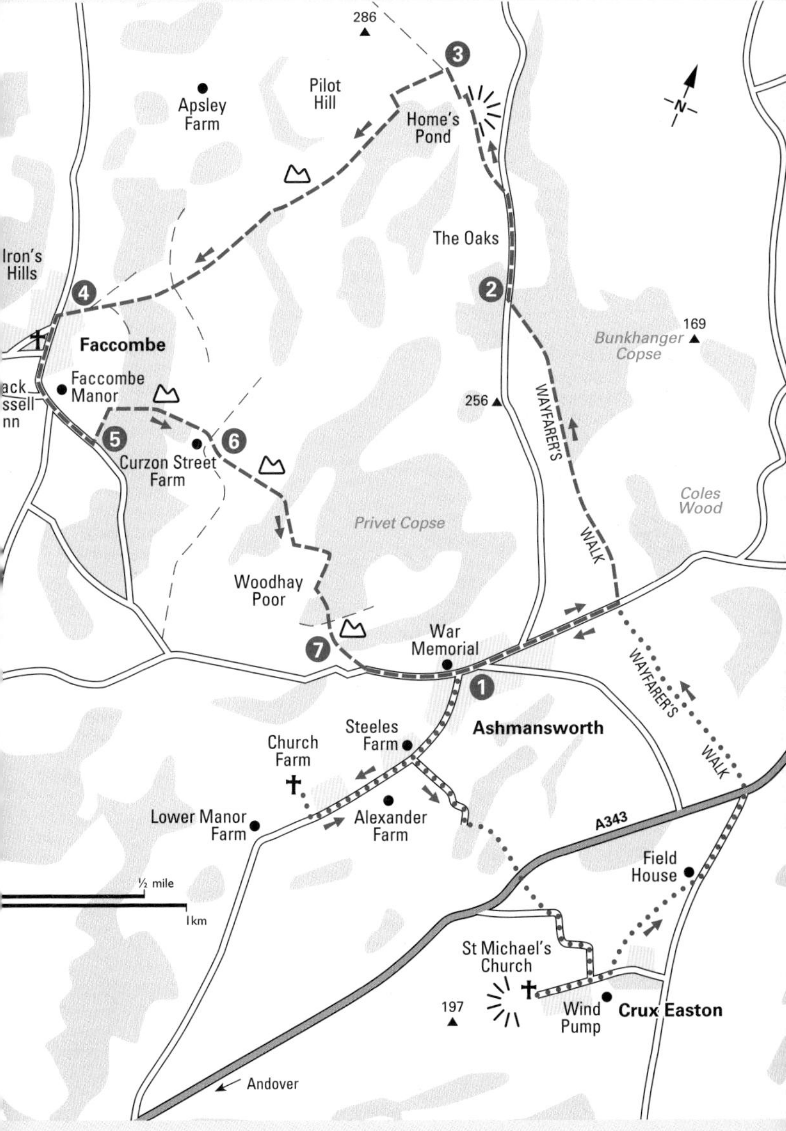

## WALK 28 DIRECTIONS

1 Walk north along the village street, keeping ahead at the fork, signed to Newbury. In 0.25 mile (400m), just before you reach a house, turn left along a byway (Wayfarers Walk – WW). Keep to this ancient track along the ridge and beside Bunkhanger Copse to a lane.

2 Turn right and savour the far-reaching views north. In 0.25 mile (400m), bear off left with a WW marker, just before lane begins to descend. Follow the stony track along the ridge, bearing left then right to cross open downland to a crossing of paths.

3 Cross the stile on your left and head straight across pasture (this is Pilot Hill) to a stile. Bear left along the field-edge, crossing two more stiles, then turn right on to a stony track alongside woodland. Steeply descend into a combe, keep ahead at a crossing of tracks and gradually climb, the track eventually merging with a metalled lane.

4 Bear right into Faccombe and turn left along the village street. Pass the church and a lane on your right, signed to the Jack Russell Inn, then turn left (signed 'Ashmansworth') by the side of Faccombe Manor. In 200yds (183m), take the arrowed path left beside double gates.

5 Keep to the left-hand field-edge, following the track right, and steeply descend through woodland. At a junction of tracks, bear right to pass two brick and flint farm buildings (Curzon Street Farm).

6 Proceed straight ahead at the crossing of tracks and keep to the main track as it steeply ascends the valley side into woodland. Emerge from the trees and keep to the track beside Privet Copse. Continue ahead at a junction of tracks, across the field and a track to join a narrow path (marked by a yellow arrow on a post) through a copse.

7 Drop down on to a track, bear left, then immediately right and steeply climb to a gap beside a gate. Turn left along a lane, following it uphill into Ashmansworth.

### WHAT TO LOOK OUT FOR

In Crux Easton, on the shorter Walk 29, look out for the unusual metal wind pump. Designed to pump water to the manor house, it is believed to be the only remaining pump of its kind in southern England.

### WHILE YOU'RE THERE

Visit the beautiful, unrestored Church of St James in Ashmansworth. Look for the 14th-century wall paintings and for the grave of Gerald Finzi, the composer, who lived in the village from 1939 to his death in 1956. He was best known for his music set to poetry and his place in English music is honoured here in the memorial window in the porch, engraved by Lawrence Whistler.

### WHERE TO EAT AND DRINK

At the half way point in Faccombe you will find an extensive menu at the Jack Russell Inn.

# Green Lanes to Crux Easton



*A shorter walk from Ashmansworth visits little Crux Easton and uses the network of ancient green lanes.*

**See map and information panel for Walk 28**

**DISTANCE** *4 miles (6.4km)* **MINIMUM TIME** *1hr 45min*

**ASCENT/GRADIENT** *225ft (69m)* ▲▲▲ **LEVEL OF DIFFICULTY** +++

## WALK 29 DIRECTIONS (Walk 28 option)

At the green and war memorial, turn right and follow the lane to the church. Return along the lane and take the footpath right, opposite Steele's Farm. Cross two stiles and walk down the left-hand field-edge over a third stile. Bear right with the field-edge, cross a stile on your left and descend through a copse to a stile. Climb uphill, soon to bear half right across the field to a stile. Descend to and cross the A343. Maintain direction across the field to a gateway in the trees. In a few paces, keep left along a track, passing two properties before climbing to a crossroads in Crux Easton. Turn right to St Michael's Church.

Tiny Crux Easton may look undistinguished in appearance but it hides a rich and varied past. First recorded in the 11th century as Estune, it then became Eston Croc, after Croc the huntsman, a warden of Chute Forest who held the manor in 1086. By 1692 the manor belonged to the Lisle family. Edward Lisle wrote a best-selling book on agriculture, *Observations in Husbandry*, which was published by his son in 1757, 30 years after his father's death.

You will find St Michael's Church a simple, yet delightful Georgian building. Built in 1775 on the site of a Norman church, it contains the original font, lectern and pulpit and there are splendid views south across Hampshire from the churchyard. A former rector of the church between 1897 and 1921 was Charles de Havilland, whose son Geoffrey became the famous aircraft designer and manufacturer. It was at nearby Highclere that he built his first aircraft, making his inaugural flight from nearby Beacon Hill in 1909.

The former rectory was later used during the Second World War to intern Sir Oswald Mosley, founder of the black-shirted British Union of Fascists.

Return to the crossroads, turn left, then immediately right over a stile. Cross the field and skirt a farm, then proceed across a field to the road by Field House. Turn left and follow the road to the junction with the A343. Turn left then, opposite Three Legged Cross, cross the road to join the Wayfarers Walk. Keep to this path along the ridge, which can be extremely muddy in winter, to a lane. Turn left and walk back into Ashmansworth.

# Water-Powered Mills from Whitchurch

*Combine a stroll through the infant Test Valley, famous for its specialised paper-making mills, with a visit to a working silk mill.*

**DISTANCE** *5.5 miles (8.8km)* **MINIMUM TIME** *2hrs30min*

**ASCENT/GRADIENT** *90ft (27m)* ▲▲▲ **LEVEL OF DIFFICULTY** +++

**PATHS** *Riverside paths, field-edge paths and road, 11 stiles*

**LANDSCAPE** *Town streets and farmland*

**SUGGESTED MAP** *OS Explorer 144 Basingstoke, Alton & Whitchurch*

**START / FINISH** *Grid reference: SU 463478*

**DOG FRIENDLINESS** *Keep dogs until control at all times*

**PARKING** *Car park next to Whitchurch Silk Mill on Winchester Street*

**PUBLIC TOILETS** *Bell Street, Whitchurch*

## WALK 30 DIRECTIONS

First established as a borough and a market in the 13th century, due to its location at a crossing point on the River Test and a junction of two major routes, the small town of Whitchurch was at its most important during the coaching era when it was the first overnight stop out of London. Industry, in the form of mills, flourished in the town and along the Test, utilising the river to provide power before electricity. The Silk Mill, which straddles the Test, survives and is a splendid example of industrial architecture. Built in 1815 on the site of previous mills, it was used for hand-weaving wool before switching to silk weaving around 1830.

You can visit the Silk Mill before or after your walk. But it is not the only mill you will see along the route. The iron-free water of the infant Test is ideal for paper making, notably for the manufacture of watermarked banknote paper.

Turn right along the road, then right again at 'The Weir'. Cross the stream and take the footpath right over the River Test and beside the river. Bear sharp left up to All Hallows Church and the main road. Turn right for the village centre. At the roundabout, take the road to the right of the White Hart Hotel, signed 'Overton'. In 0.25 mile (400m), turn right down 'The Green', the road narrowing to a track. Keep to the left-hand edge of water-meadows. Bear left through a hedge and follow the right-hand field-edge, which soon swings left beside the River Test. Cross a stile and bear half left across a field to

**WHILE YOU'RE THERE**

Visit the Silk Mill, now a working museum, and take a trip back in time to the days of water power and flying shuttles. See the restored Victorian machinery and weavers working the looms which turn the silk into luxury fabrics for theatrical costumes, historic houses and Britain's top barristers.

a metalled drive. Turn right, cross the bridge above Bere Mill and keep left at a fork of footpaths to a stile.

Henri Portal, a Huguenot from France, first established his paper-making business at Bere Mill in 1712. This attractive weatherboarded mill, although no longer in commercial use, has has changed little since Portal occupied it.

Bear half right across the field to a stile and keep ahead along the right-hand field boundary. Follow the path to the right of cottages and down a metalled track, following it left by the church, then right over the Test to the B3400. Turn left here for 200yds (183m) for the Watership Down pub; otherwise turn right and cross the river. Turn right, opposite the former Laverstoke Mill, along Laverstoke Lane.

Portal moved to his new mill at Laverstoke in 1724 where he started making the watermarked paper for banknotes. Portals had and still have a monopoly in this specialised type of paper. The original contract with the Bank of England survives to this day. The business remained in Laverstoke until 1950, when it moved to a mill in nearby Overton which Portals had opened in 1922. Much of the estate village was built by Portals for its workers. Look out for the unusual row of half-thatched cottages, built in 1939 in an Arts and Crafts style, and the finely built, ochre-coloured Laverstoke House, built in 1796 for Harry Portal.

Pass the sports and social club, then take the second path right along a track. Climb steadily, then as it turns sharp right, bear left into a field and follow the field-edge left to a gap in the far corner. Walk along the left-hand edge of two fields. Gradually descend to the stile in the corner, and continue beside the woods to a further stile. Keep ahead beneath a steep bank on your left, cross a stile, and continue along the right-hand field-edge of three fields. Join a metalled footpath, pass the school gate and skirt the playing fields. Follow McFauld Way and turn right along a track, beside playing fields. Cross the road back into the car park.

### WHERE TO EAT AND DRINK

Whitchurch has a good choice of good pubs, notably the Red House Inn and the White Hart Hotel, a 15th-century coaching inn. Home-made lunches, tea and coffee are available in the Silk Mill Tearoom (admission charge). The Watership Down Inn at Freefolk offers a full restaurant-style menu.

### WHAT TO LOOK FOR

All Hallows Church in Whitchurch has some interesting memorials, particularly a fine brass of Richard Brooke and family (1603), complete with a rhyming epitaph, and a rare 9th-century Saxon gravestone with a carving of Christ. It is believed to be from the tomb of a woman named Frithburga, a nun from nearby Wherwell. The Latin inscription reads: 'Here lies the body Frithburga, buried in peace', and for generations bell-ringers used the stone to stand on before realising its significance. A classical reredos and a 15th-century wooden screen that forms the front of a family pew survive in the tiny rustic Church of St Nicholas at Freefolk.

WALK 31

# High Above Highclere Castle

*From a hilltop grave on Beacon Hill, to a uniquely decorated chapel.*

**DISTANCE** *7 miles (11.3km)* **MINIMUM TIME** *3hrs 30min*

**ASCENT/GRADIENT** *767ft (234m)* ▲▲▲ **LEVEL OF DIFFICULTY** +++

**PATHS** *Tracks, field and woodland paths, some roads, 5 stiles*

**LANDSCAPE** *Open downland and farmland, with patches of woodland*

**SUGGESTED MAP** *OS Explorers 144 Basingstoke, Alton & Whitchurch; 158 Newbury & Hungerford*

**START / FINISH** *Grid reference: SU 463576 (on Explorer 144)*

**DOG FRIENDLINESS** *Off lead on Beacon Hill, otherwise keep under control*

**PARKING** *Beacon Hill car park off A34*

**PUBLIC TOILETS** *None en route*

Due to the steep gradient leading to the summit of Beacon Hill, the highest point of the North Hampshire Downs at 857ft (261m), it's advisable to climb the hill at the start of your walk! Unless you're walking this route in July or August and plan to include the spur to Highclere Castle, don't miss the Earl of Carnarvon's grave and the views across the Highclere Estate.

Set within a landscape of parkland and wooded hills designed by 'Capability' Brown during 1774–77, Highclere Castle is a magnificent pastiche of a medieval castle, impressively grand inside and out. But Hampshire's largest mansion is early Victorian, designed and built in neo-Elizabethan style by Charles Barry, architect of the Houses of Parliament, between 1839 and 1842 around an earlier house. It is the home of the Earls of Carnarvon and the sumptuous interior, particularly the great hall, the library, the Rococo-style drawing room, and the dining room, are adorned with fine portraits of the Earl's family, the Herberts.

Of the seven Earls of Carnarvon that have resided at Highclere, it is the 5th and probably the best known that we are interested in. George Herbert had been fascinated by Egypt and archaeology from an early age and it was following a serious accident in 1902 that he spent time recuperating in the country. From 1906 he began sponsoring archaeological investigations, employing Howard Clark, an expert Egyptologist. In 1922, after years of hard work excavating in the Valley of Kings near Thebes, they discovered the tomb of Tutenkahmun and treasures that had been buried for over 3,000 years. The 5th Earl died a year later from an infected mosquito bite, an event which led to the stories of the curse of Tutenkahmun. His body was brought back to England and, as instructed, he was buried at the top of Beacon Hill overlooking his beloved estate. Sadly, much of the 5th Earl's collection was sold after his death, but some artefacts were discovered in a hiding place in the castle in 1987 and you can see these on display. Unfortunately, outside July and August, you will have to be content with viewing the impressive castle and grounds from the 5th Earl's grave on Beacon Hill or on television as the location for *Downton Abbey*.

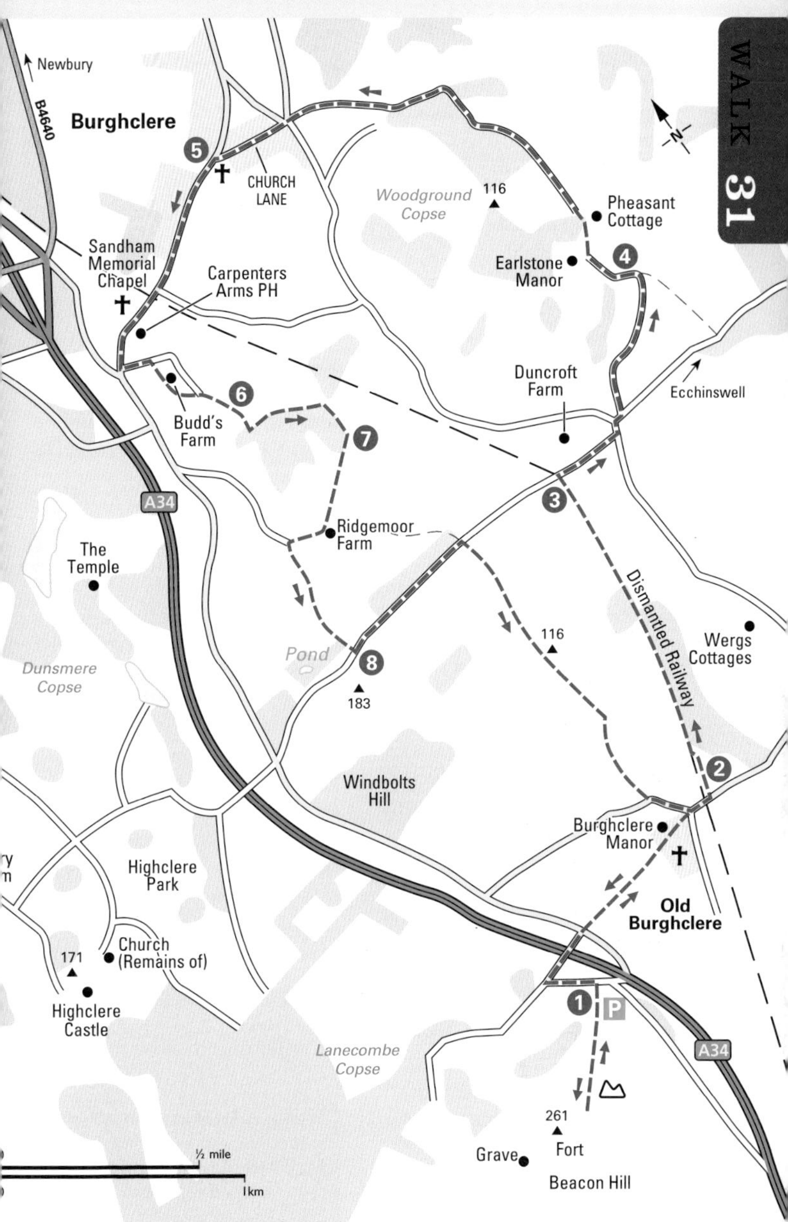


## WALK 31 DIRECTIONS

**1** Climb Beacon Hill at the start or finish of the walk. Leave the car park via the access road and cross the A34 bridge to reach a T-junction. Take the footpath opposite, downhill to a gate and walk along the field-edge to Old Burghclere. Pass beside the churchyard wall and Burghclere Manor to a lane. Proceed ahead, cross the old railway bridge and take the path left.

❷ Keep to the left-hand field-edge and enter woodland. In a few steps, bear left on to the old trackbed. Turn right and follow the track and later a narrow path for 0.5 mile (800m) to a bridge.

❸ Bear left up a chalky path to a track and turn right over the bridge. Gently descend to a lane, turn left and then right, signed 'Ecchinswell'. In 50yds (46m), take the waymarked bridleway left. Keep to this tree-lined path to a gravel drive and turn left.

❹ Follow the track through the grounds of Earlstone Manor, passing ponds and Pheasant Cottage. Proceed through or close to woodland for a mile (1.6km) to a road. Keep ahead along Church Lane in Burghclere, signed to Sandham Memorial Chapel.

**WHILE YOU'RE THERE**

Visit the Sandham Memorial Chapel (cared for by the National Trust) in Burghclere. Built in the 1920s, the interior walls are entirely covered with magnificent paintings by the artist Stanley Spencer between 1926 and 1932. They depict the everyday grind and routine of a soldier's life during the Great War.

❺ Turn left by the church and keep to the road, continuing past the Memorial Chapel and the Carpenters Arms, before turning left along a metalled dead-end lane. Pass Ashold Farm, then take the footpath right between gardens to a stile. Skirt round Budd's Farm across three fields via three more stiles and join a path through trees to a stile.

❻ Turn right along the field-edge, following it left in the corner. Drop down to a fingerpost and turn right along a boardwalk into woodland. At a broken stile, turn right along the woodland edge, then right again over a plank bridge to a gate.

**WHAT TO LOOK OUT FOR**

Climb the steep grassy slopes of Beacon Hill (covered in cowslips in spring) to view the Iron Age hill fort close to its highest point. The well-preserved single rampart and ditch enclose the site of around 20 huts. Just inside the defences is the grave of the 5th Earl of Carnarvon, who died in 1923.

❼ Keep ahead across the pasture towards Ridgemoor Farm. Pass a pond to a gate and track. Turn right, then where it bears right, turn left up a wooded sunken path to a track.

❽ Turn left to a crossroads and turn right. Head uphill and keep to the undulating track for 0.5mile (800m) to Old Burghclere. Turn left along the lane and then right along the drive to Old Burghclere Manor. Retrace your outward steps back to the Beacon Hill car park.

**WHERE TO EAT AND DRINK**

In Burghclere, at the half way point, is the Carpenters Arms, a homely pub offering bar food, Arkells ales and a sunny rear terrace with rural views. Highclere Castle has a restaurant and tea room.



*Right: Highclere Castle (located close to Walk 31)*

# Hampshire's Great Garden at Exbury



*Combine a delightful walk along the Solent foreshore with a visit to a magnificent woodland garden on the banks of the Beaulieu River.*

**DISTANCE** *6.5 miles (10.4km)* **MINIMUM TIME** *3hrs*

**ASCENT/GRADIENT** *114ft (35m)* ▲▲▲ **LEVEL OF DIFFICULTY** +++

**PATHS** *Fields, woodland and foreshore paths, some roads, 4 stiles*

**LANDSCAPE** *Coastline and farmland dotted with woodland*

**SUGGESTED MAP** *OS Explorer OL 22 New Forest*

**START / FINISH** *Grid reference: SZ 455985*

**DOG FRIENDLINESS** *Keep dogs under control at all times*

**PARKING** *Pay-and-display car parks at Lepe Country Park*

**PUBLIC TOILETS** *Lepe Country Park and Exbury Gardens*

With its shingle beaches, wild natural habitats and clumps of pine trees, Lepe Country Park is a perfect place to begin exploring one of the remote and most beautiful stretches of the Hampshire coast. It affords superb views across the Solent to the Isle of Wight and provides an excellent vantage point to watch passing yachts and ships, in particular huge tankers making their way to the oil refinery at nearby Fawley. To the west lie silent and eerie mudflats and marshland expanses at the mouth of the Beaulieu River and the fine gardens at Exbury, the focus of our walk.

## Outstanding Gardens

Exbury is a rare surviving example of an estate village and enjoys an enviable position, being peacefully situated on the edge of the New Forest and just 1 mile (1.6km) from the Solent coast. Pride of place in the village goes to Exbury House and its 200 acres (81ha) of landscaped woodland gardens which lie on the sheltered east bank of the beautiful Beaulieu River. The gardens were the life's work of Lionel de Rothschild, a member of the banking family, who bought the estate in 1919. Having extended the early 19th-century house he set to work in establishing one of the most outstanding rhododendron gardens in the world.

The acid rich soil already supported fine specimens of oak, great cedars and Wellingtonias which provided the perfect backdrop for the rhododendrons and other acid-loving plants, including azaleas, camellias and magnolias. Today, nearly 80 years on, the gardens are internationally famous for rhododendrons and azaleas and over 1,200 hybrids have been created. A network of tracks enables you to explore the countless plantings, the cascades and ponds, a rose garden, heather garden and iris garden, daffodil meadow and a delightful walk along the banks of the river with views across to Bucklers Hard.

Exbury provides a feast of visual delights all year round and you should allow at least two hours for a visit, especially in the spring and autumn. Stroll through the gardens in late spring and the vibrant colours of the rhododendrons and azaleas will be mesmerising.

*Left: Exbury Gardens, New Forest National Park (Walk 32)*

On a warm summer's day, head for the garden to experience the amazing range of blooms and botanical rarities, while high summer is the perfect time to saunter and relax in the shade of the great trees, including ancient, awe-inspiring yews, and admire the peace and beauty of Exbury. In the autumn, the beautiful specimen trees will reward you with a magnificent display of purples, bronzes and mellow brown colours. Whenever you visit, you will discover that Exbury is truly a garden for all seasons.

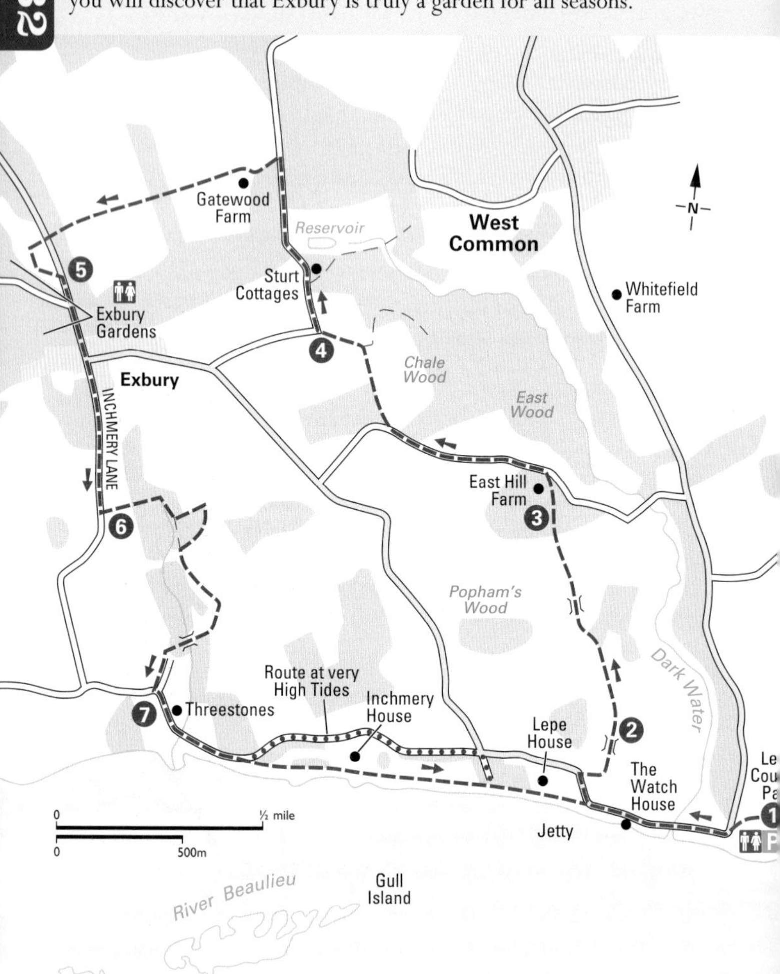


## WALK 32 DIRECTIONS

❶ Walk west from the shore car park along the road. Keep left along the path above the foreshore, and pass the distinctive black-and-white painted Watch House. Then, at a small lighthouse, turn right to meet the lane. Turn left then, as the road curves left, cross the stile on the right. Walk along the field-edge, then bear left over a bridge.

❷ Keep alongside the fence to a stile and proceed straight across the field. Briefly pass beside some woodland and follow the path to a gap in the hedge near a telegraph pole. Follow the path across the next field and into the woodland ahead. Continue through the trees, bearing right beyond a footbridge, then right with waymarker post to join a fenced bridleway arrowed to the left.

**3** Pass East Hill Farm, and walk along the gravelled farm track until it curves sharp left. Turn right through a gate. Follow the wide path ahead, bear right on entering a field and follow the field-edge to T-junction. Turn left to a stile and lane.

**4** Turn right, continue through a gate beside a cattle grid and take the footpath left through a gate (by another cattle grid) to join a track to Gatewood Farm. Bear right at the fork, walk around the farm complex, and remain on the track for 0.75 mile (1.2km) to a gate and lane. Go straight across for Exbury Gardens (where there's a tea room).

### WHERE TO EAT AND DRINK

Lepe Country Park has a seasonal restaurant and refreshment kiosk. There's also a licensed restaurant, with no access charge, offering coffee, good light lunches and teas at Exbury Gardens. Delicious teas can be had at the Tennis Court Tea Garden if you're exploring Exbury in high summer.

**5** On leaving Exbury Gardens, turn right along the road then, where the road bends left, keep ahead, signed 'Inchmery Lane". Continue to a waymarked path and stile on the left.

**6** Cross the stile and walk straight across grassland into woodland, following the path right, through the trees. At a crossing of paths, turn left over a

### WHAT TO LOOK OUT FOR

Walk to the eastern extent of Lepe Country Park to see some relics from of the Second World War. The extensive raised concrete platforms are all that remain of the construction site of the floating 'Mulberry' harbours that were towed across to Normandy for the D-Day landings in June 1944.

plank bridge. On leaving the trees, turn right along the field-edge beside the woodland to a gap in the hedge near a 3-way signpost. Keep the woodland edge on your right until the path bears right over a footbridge into the woods. Two more footbridges lead out through a kissing gate to a lane.

**7** Turn left and follow the lane to the shore. Proceed along the foreshore (follow the fingerpost) close to the high tide line and continue below Inchmery House. Pass Lepe House and rejoin your outward route past The Watch House back to Lepe Country Park. The final stretch along the foreshore may be impassable at high tide, so keep to the lane around Inchmery House, then, just before the road junction, turn right beside a barrier down to the foreshore to pick up the path past Lepe House.

### WHILE YOU'RE THERE

Visit Calshot Castle. Down past the oil refineries and power stations east of Lepe you will find this Tudor fort, built for Henry VIII on the spit beyond the tidal flats of Southampton Water. There are excellent Solent views and an exhibition tells the story of the former flying boat base, which is now the County's outdoor pursuits centre.

# New Forest Trails

*Ancient oaks, historic inclosures and exotic towering conifers in the New Forest.*

DISTANCE *8 miles (12.9km)* MINIMUM TIME *4hrs*

ASCENT/GRADIENT *318ft (97m)* ▲▲▲ LEVEL OF DIFFICULTY +++

PATHS *Grass and gravel forest tracks, heathland paths, some roads*

LANDSCAPE *Ornamental Drive, ancient forest inclosures and heathland*

SUGGESTED MAP *OS Explorer OL 22 New Forest*

START / FINISH *Grid reference: SU 266057*

DOG FRIENDLINESS *Keep dogs under control at all times*

PARKING *Brock Hill Forestry Commission car park, just off A35*

PUBLIC TOILETS *Blackwater car park*

A short drive south-west of Lyndhurst are ancient woods of oak and beech, notably Bolderwood, and the impressive, mid-19th century conifer plantation of the Rhinefield Ornamental Drive. Here you are in the true heart of the New Forest and this fascinating loop walk explores these contrasting landscapes. The shorter loop (Walk 34) is a relaxing stroll through the rhododendron-lined Ornamental Drive, with its magnificent tall trees and arboretum, while the longer option takes you through the forest's finest unenclosed and 'inclosed' deciduous woods. Link the two together for a memorable 10-mile (16km) ramble.

### Finest Relics of Woodland

Unenclosed woodlands such as Whitley Wood are among the finest relics of unspoilt deciduous forest in Western Europe. Hummocky green lawns and paths meander beneath giant beech trees and beside stands of ancient holly and contorted oaks, and through peaceful, sunny glades edged with elegant silver birch. 'Inclosures' are areas of managed woodlands where young trees are protected from deer and ponies. Areas of oak trees were first inclosed in the late 17th century to provide the huge quantities of timber required by the construction and shipbuilding industries. Holidays Hill Inclosure is one of the forest's oldest, dating from 1676. Here you'll find some 300-year-old oak trees that matured after iron replaced wood in the shipbuilding industry.

You will pass the most famous and probably the oldest tree in the forest, the Knightwood Oak, soon after beginning the longer walk. Believed to be 350 years old, it owes its great age to pollarding (cutting back) its limbs to encourage new branches for fuel and charcoal. Pollarding was made illegal in 1698 as full-grown trees were needed to provide timber for shipbuilding, so any oak or beech tree that show signs of having been pollarded is of a great age. Marvel at the girth of this fine oak, a massive 24ft (7.3m), before walking through Holidays Hill Inclosure.

Close to Millyford Bridge and Highland Water stands the Portugese Fireplace, a memorial to the work of a Portugese Army unit, deployed during the First World War to cut timber for pit-props. The flint fireplace was used in their cookhouse. Returning through Holidays Hill Inclosure you will join a 'reptile trail' and several marker posts, each carved with a different type of British reptile, lead you to the New Forest reptillary. Set up to breed rarer species for the wild, including the smooth snake and sand lizard, it offers you the opportunity to view some of the forest's more elusive inhabitants. Visit on a hot sunny day, when these cold blooded creatures are more active, and you will see the venomous adder, the olive green grass snake, common lizards and the rare natterjack toad.

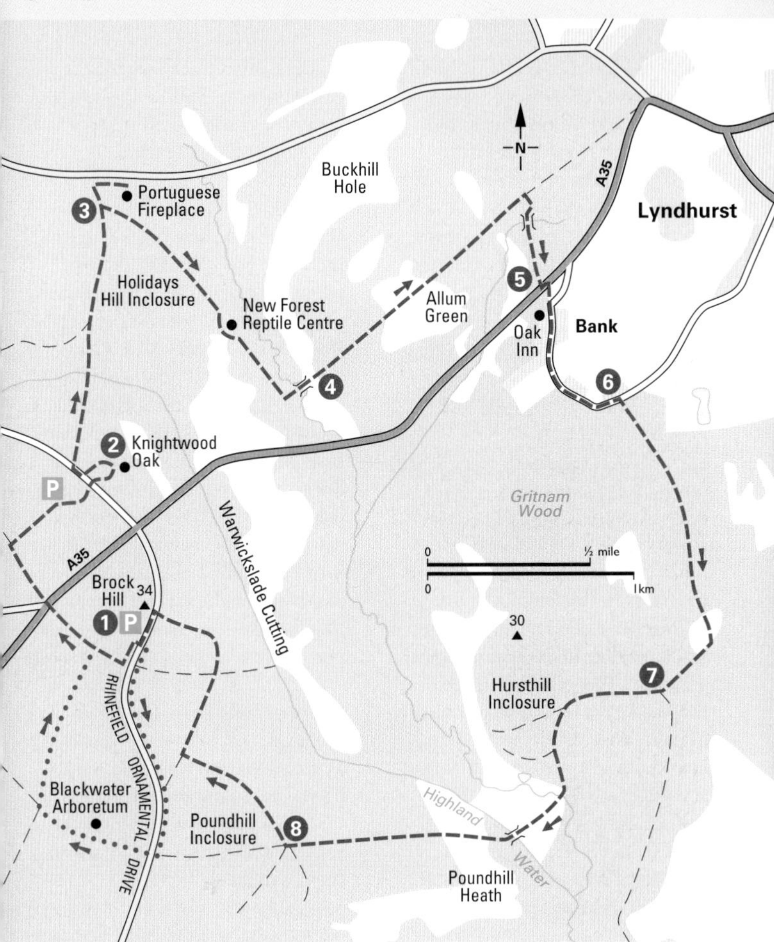


## WALK 33 DIRECTIONS

**1** Take the gravel path at the southern end of the car park (beyond the information post), parallel with the road. In 100yds (91m) turn right just before a bench seat and descend to a gravel track. Cross straight over; then, where the path curves left, keep ahead to reach a gate and the A35. Cross over the A35 (take care), go through a gate and keep to the path, uphill to a junction. Turn right and follow the path to Knightwood Oak car park, then follow the sign to the Knightwood Oak itself.

❷ Return towards the car park and bear right along the road. Turn right again after a few paces, on to a path into mixed woodland. Cross a stream and soon reach a gravel track. Bear right and keep to this trail, passing red marker posts, to a fork. Keep left to reach a gate and road. Turn right to view the Portuguese Fireplace.

❸ Return through Holidays Hill Inclosure to the fork of tracks. Bear left and follow this to the New Forest Reptile Centre. Walk along the access drive past a cottage dated 1811 then, at a barrier on your left, drop down on to a path and follow it across a bridge.

**WHERE TO EAT AND DRINK**

You may find an ice cream van in Blackwater car park on Walk 34. On Walk 33, aim to make it to the Oak in Bank for lunch. A traditional pub, it offers ale from the cask, and decent food.

❹ Keep to the main path for 0.75 mile (1.2km), skirting the walls to Allum Green and several clearings, then gently climb through trees to a defined crossing of paths and turn right. Shortly, bear half right across a clearing and concrete footbridge, then continue through the woodland edge to an electricity pole. Bear right for 20yds (18m), then left through a gate to the A35.

❺ Turn left, then almost immediately right across the road to a gate. Walk ahead to a garden boundary and turn right, the narrow path leading to a lane in Bank. Turn right, pass the Oak Inn and walk through the hamlet.

❻ Just beyond the cattle grid, turn right through a gate on to a gravelled track towards Brockenhurst. Follow this track for nearly a mile (1.4km) to a junction at a small green.

**WHAT TO LOOK FOR**

More than 4,000 New Forest ponies graze the lawns and trees on the heath and scrub near Allum Green and Poundhill Heath. They are descendants of a wild breed peculiar to the New Forest and belong to local commoners.

❼ Fork right towards Brockenhurst, and enter Hursthill Inclosure at a gate. Drop down past a turning on the right, then climb again and bear left at a fork. Keep to the waymarked track as it drops past another turning on the right and leaves Hursthill Inclosure at a gate. Walk the long straight track to the bridge over Highland Water, and follow the track round to the right. Soon a gate leads the waymarked trail into Poundhill Inclosure, and another straight section brings you to a five-way junction at waymark post 24.

❽ Turn right here. Ignore all turnings, and follow the track as it turns sharp right and winds its way to a junction with the Ornamental Drive. Turn left for the last 100 yards (91m) back to the car park.

**WHILE YOU'RE THERE**

Visit the New Forest Centre in Lyndhurst which brings to life the history, traditions and wildlife of the New Forest. Take a trip up the Bolderwood Ornamental Drive and visit the deer sanctuary near Bolderwood car park.

# Rhinefield Ornamental Drive



*A short loop round the impressive 19th-century plantation.*

**See map and information panel for Walk 33**

**DISTANCE** *1.75 miles (2.8km)* **MINIMUM TIME** *1hr*

**ASCENT/GRADIENT** *49ft (15m)* ▲▲▲ **LEVEL OF DIFFICULTY** +++

## WALK 34 DIRECTIONS (Walk 33 option)

At the bottom of the Rhinefield Ornamental Drive stands the Rhinefield House Hotel, a flamboyant Jacobean-style house, built in 1890 on the site of a hunting lodge used by Charles II. Magnificent gardens surround the mansion and rhododendrons and azaleas line the ornamental carriage drive, until 1938 a gravel track, that links the house with the A35. Planted informally in the mid-19th century with exotic trees such as Wellingtonias, redwoods, black spruce and Spanish fir, the Ornamental Drive has reached maturity and some of the trees are the largest of their species in Britain. This short circular trail passes some of these fine specimens.

Locate the Tall Trees Trail post at the southern end of the car park and follow the gravel path to the road and cross straight over. Keep to the gravel trail (marked by white-banded posts) as it curves right and runs parallel with the road. Pass through an impressive mixed wooded area, featuring tall Douglas firs, one of which is over 150ft (46m) tall, Norwegian spruces, and displays of rhododendrons in early summer. One of the giant Wellingtonias is 160ft (50m) tall but in its native California it can grow to twice that height!

The path meanders gently downhill to Blackwater car park, passing several sculptured information panels along the way.

At the car park, turn right through the rustic arch, cross the road and follow the track towards the Arboretum. (Turn right if you wish to explore the Tall Trees Trail further and return to the track.) Go through a gate into the arboretum. Although not a large area, it is well worth exploring the various paths that criss-cross the arboretum, passing labelled trees and welcome benches, where you can rest and enjoy the peace and quiet. Exit by the far gate and keep to the gravel track to a crossing of tracks. Turn right and remain on this track over a low summit and crossways to a crossing of paths. (Turn left here to join Walk 33). Turn right uphill, then on reaching a gravel path, turn left back to the car park.

# Beaulieu to Bucklers Hard

*Step back in time on this riverside stroll through the Beaulieu Estate.*

**DISTANCE** *4.75 miles (7.7km)* **MINIMUM TIME** *2hrs 30mins*

**ASCENT/GRADIENT** *Negligible* ▲▲▲ **LEVEL OF DIFFICULTY** +++

**PATHS** *Tracks, field, woodland and riverside paths*

**LANDSCAPE** *River valley with woodland, farmland and marshes*

**SUGGESTED MAP** *OS Explorer OL 22 New Forest*

**START / FINISH** *Grid reference: SU 386021*

**DOG FRIENDLINESS** *Let them off lead on woodland paths*

**PARKING** *Pay-and-display car park in Beaulieu village*

**PUBLIC TOILETS** *Beaulieu and Bucklers Hard*

## WALK 35 DIRECTIONS

Idyllically set at the head of the Beaulieu River, historic Beaulieu is an attractive village of red-brick Georgian cottages dominated by Palace House, originally the great gatehouse to a Cistercian abbey founded in 1204 by King John. To many visitors, Beaulieu is just the abbey ruins and the famous motor museum, but, despite its overwhelming popularity, the village remains relatively unspoilt and is well worth exploring.

From the bottom of the village street, bear right past the Montagu Arms Hotel and take the waymarked Solent Way along the gravel track beside the hotel.

**WHERE TO EAT AND DRINK**

In Bucklers Hard you will find the Captain's Café and the Master Builder's House Hotel (Yachtsmen's Bar open all day), the latter offering good bar food. In Beaulieu, try the Old Bakehouse Tearooms or Monty's for real ale and pub food.

Continue round the hotel car parks to a gate. With views across the Beaulieu River, remain on the track past an inlet, then through Jarvis's Copse and along the left-hand side of a field to Brickyard Cottage at Bailey's Hard.

Bailey's Hard was formerly the site of a thriving brick-making industry in the 18th century. Bricks were made here until the 1930s and many were used in the construction of the estate houses. It was also where the first naval vessel to be built on the Beaulieu River, the *Salisbury*, was completed in 1698.

Continue along the track. Shortly, bear right, then left along the track, signed to Bucklers Hard. Stay on this path through Keeping Copse for 0.75 mile (1.2km).

Keeping Copse was replanted in about 1820, after much of the mature timber had been felled for shipbuilding. You can still identify some of the trees that were encouraged to grow the heavy side branches used in the ship's frames.

**WHILE YOU'RE THERE**

Take a cruise on the tranquil Beaulieu River from Bucklers Hard and view the abundant birdlife on the salt marshes. On your return to Beaulieu, visit Palace House, the home of Lord Montagu, and the adjacent remains of the 13th-century abbey with its exhibition on monastic life. If time allows, take a look at the famous National Motor Museum.

At a small car park, go through the gate ahead and follow the track right. Bear left at the entrance to the *Agamemnon* boatyard, follow the signposted route to the water's edge, and continue to the quay in Bucklers Hard.

The timeless village of Bucklers Hard, with its single picturesque wide street leading down to the river, was laid out during the 18th century by the 2nd Duke of Montagu. Having been granted the West Indian islands of St Lucia and St Vincent, he envisaged developing his own port on the Beaulieu River to import and refine sugar grown on the islands. Sadly, his dream was shattered when the French invaded his islands. Twenty years later, having inherited the right to have a free harbour and due to the proximity of plentiful timber supplies, Bucklers Hard became a prosperous shipbuilding centre. Many of the early wooden warships, including Nelson's HMS *Agamemnon*, were made from New Forest oak here until the company was dissolved in around 1820. In its busy days the wide main street would have been used for rolling great logs to the 'hard' where the ships were built. Today, the whole village is a living museum, the street is free of traffic and the village scene remains exactly as it was in its shipbuilding heyday. While you're here, visit the Maritime Museum and learn about the shipbuilding industry through fascinating displays, large-scale models and various artifacts, including items from the voyages of Sir Francis Chichester who moored his yacht here. Then, explore authentically reconstructed cottage and inn interiors and gain an insight into the life of the workers in the 18th century, before strolling along the river bank to view the remains of the inlets where some of the 50 wooden naval and merchant vessels were built.

Return along the river bank, past the *Agamemnon* boatyard. Fork right, signed 'Beaulieu via Riverside Walk', to follow a delightful woodland path walking beside the tidal river. This eventually joins the main woodland path you followed on the outward route. Turn right and retrace your steps past Brickyard Cottage to Beaulieu.

**WHAT TO LOOK OUT FOR**

As you walk beside the Beaulieu River look out for the waders and wildfowl, including shelduck, curlew, redshank and oystercatcher, that thrive on the tidal mudflats and salt marsh. Make a point of visiting Beaulieu Abbey Church (free access before noon), formerly the monks refectory. Note the original 13th-century stone reading pulpit, reached via a vaulted staircase, and the graves of Lady Isabella, wife of King John's son, the Earl of Cornwall who died in 1240, and that of Princess Eleana, infant daughter of Edward I.

# Church Treasures at Minstead

*Combine a varied walk through New Forest inclosures with a visit to Minstead's church, burial place of Sir Arthur Conan Doyle.*

**DISTANCE** *5.5 miles (8.8km)* **MINIMUM TIME** *2hrs 30min*

**ASCENT/GRADIENT** *361ft (110m)* ▲▲▲ **LEVEL OF DIFFICULTY** +++

**PATHS** *Field paths, bridleways, forest tracks, roads, 5 stiles*

**LANDSCAPE** *Pasture and farmland, forest inclosures and heathland*

**SUGGESTED MAP** *OS Explorer OL 22 New Forest*

**START / FINISH** *Grid reference: SU 280109*

**DOG FRIENDLINESS** *Let them off lead on heathland*

**PARKING** *Minstead church or by village green*

**PUBLIC TOILETS** *None en route*

Of the New Forest's half-dozen delightful villages, enchanting Minstead is among the most visited and the least spoiled. Completely encircled by forest, with picture-postcard thatched and weatherboarded cottages nestling in a maze of high-banked lanes, it is one of those communities which seem completely isolated from the outside world, the lush landscape of rolling pasture and scattered woodland contrasting with the ancient surrounding forest.

## Whitby in Miniature

Referred to as Mintestede – the place where mint grows – in the Domesday Book, the village has probably remained untroubled since William Rufus was killed while out hunting at nearby Canterton Glen in 1100. Crowning a little hill overlooking the village is the Church of All Saints, one of the hidden treasures of the county, which dates back to at least the 13th century. Originally thatched and looking more like a cottage, with its series of different sized gables, dormers and attractive little extensions, it has immediate appeal and time should be allowed to explore its fascinating interior and churchyard. According to Pevsner, its wealth of old furniture and fittings is surpassed only by St Mary's at Whitby, North Yorkshire. Whitby in miniature is built of traditional New Forest materials, wattle filled in with rubble and daub, with stone only spared for the arches and quoins in the main walls. Beyond the porch and the arched main doorway, ancient wooden door and deeply worn step that has seen the passing of worshippers and pilgrims for over 800 years, you will find a surprisingly intact Georgian interior.

Note the rare and unusual three-decker pulpit, made of oak and patched with pine, dating from the 17th century. The lowest deck was used by the parish clerk who said the 'Amens'; the middle deck was where the scriptures were read and the sermon was preached from the upper level. The fine nave is filled with a double tier of galleries, built in the 18th century to accommodate musicians and the growing congregation, with the plain upper gallery added to provide free seating for children and the poor of the parish. You will also find the 17th-century box pews of interest, in particular the three family pews for the local gentry, each with their own entrance and one equipped like a cosy sitting room with comfortable seating and a fireplace.

If you take a stroll around the churchyard you'll find the grave of the best-known Minstead resident, Sir Arthur Conan Doyle (1869–1930), and his wife on the south side by an oak tree. He created Sherlock Holmes and lived at nearby Bignell Wood. He refers to Minstead Church in his novel *The White Company*. Originally buried in the garden of his home in Sussex, his body was moved to Minstead after his wife died in the 1950s.

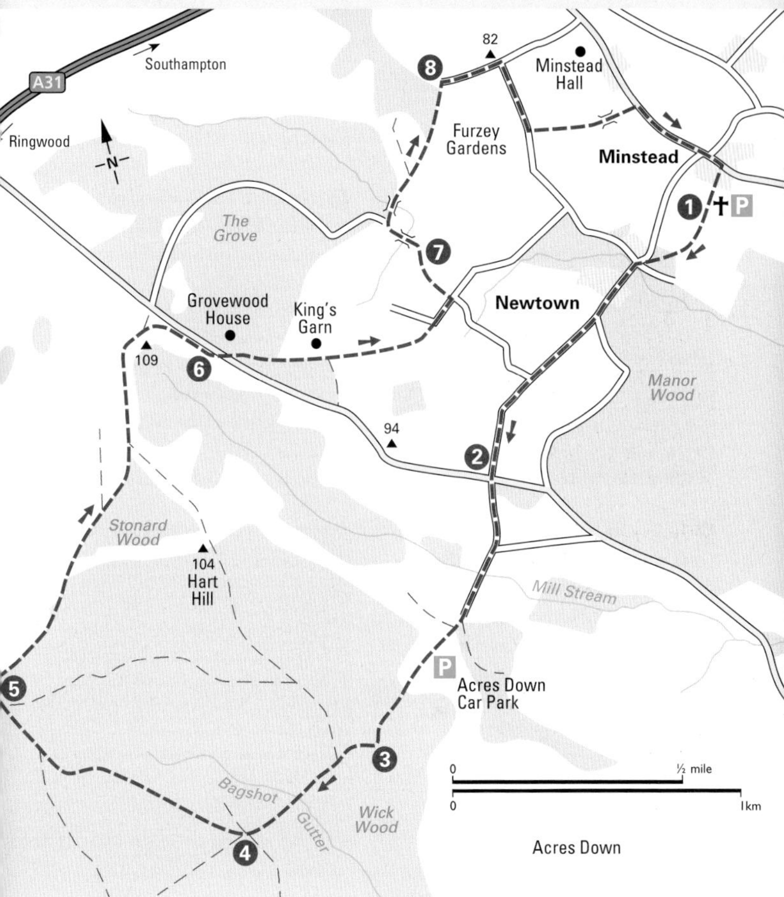


## WALK 36 DIRECTIONS

**1** Go through a gate to the right of the churchyard and walk down to another gate. Continue to enter a wood. Exit via a gate, bear right and then left on to the road. Cross the ford and keep to the lane, bearing left by a phone box.

**2** At a crossroads, go straight over, following the sign to 'Acres Down'. Cross a ford then, at the crossroads just past the farm, turn right. Almost immediately take the left fork along a track, signed 'Acres Down Car Park'. Walk past the car park and follow signposts, this time heading for Bolderwood.

3 Swing sharp right between gateposts. Ignore the junction right, cross a small stream, and continue for 380yds (347m) to a crossways and marker post.

4 Turn right, then fork immediately left and through a gate into young conifer woodland. Go through a second gate and cross a track, now walking beside mature conifers. Follow the gravel track as it bears left, then abruptly right, eventually leaving the woods via a gate.

**WHAT TO LOOK OUT FOR**

Note the unusual pub sign which depicts the 'trusty servant', a swine-snouted character with a padlocked jaw to illustrate his discretion and stags feet to indicate his speed in running errands. The original 16th-century picture and inscription (in Latin) hangs in Winchester College.

5 Bear right to walk along a track a short distance from the woodland edge, with open heath on your right. Fork left as four prominent holly trees herald the start of Stonard Wood, following the main track close to the woodland edge. Keep on the well-defined track, ignoring the routes branching left and right, for 0.5 mile (800m). Fork right through gorse and merge with a track from the right. Swing right, ignore the track branching left to the road, but keep straight on to reach the road.

6 Cross over and walk left down the verge. Pass Grovewood House and turn left down the bridleway, signed to King's Garn. Pass the house and take the left fork and join the track merging from the right. Continue downhill and just

**WHERE TO EAT AND DRINK**

The Trusty Servant in Minstead is a homely village inn offering an extensive menu, good real ale, overnight accommodation and a friendly welcome. Refreshments are available in the Craft Gallery at Furzey Gardens, and the excellent village shop in Minstead sells freshly-made sandwiches and coffee.

before reaching a road, turn left over a stile and continue between boundaries.

7 Drop down to a bridge and stile. Enter woodland and immediately turn right at a waymark post. Cross a stream, go up some steps, then fork right through a gate. Cross a plank bridge, go through a gate and continue a gentle ascent. Join a path from the right and ahead into a car park. Fork right past Furzey Gardens and down to the road.

**WHILE YOU'RE THERE**

Visit Furzey Gardens. Eight acres (3.2ha) of peaceful glades surround a restored thatched Forest cottage dating from 1560. You can see winter and summer heathers, rare flowering trees and shrubs, including flaming Chilean fire trees, extensive collections of rhododendrons and azaleas, and a wonderful display of spring bulbs. There are also displays of local arts and crafts.

8 Turn right, then right again. Take the footpath left and walk along the left-hand field-edge to a bridge and stile. Maintain direction through the next field to a road. Turn right into Minstead, then right after the pub back to the church.

# Around Roman Rockbourne



*Roman discoveries link Rockbourne and Whitsbury, by the Wiltshire border.*

**DISTANCE** *4.5 miles (7.2km)* **MINIMUM TIME** *2hrs 15min*

**ASCENT/GRADIENT** *295ft (90m)* ▲▲▲ **LEVEL OF DIFFICULTY** +++

**PATHS** *Field paths, woodland bridleways and tracks, 9 stiles*

**LANDSCAPE** *Rolling fields, areas of woodland*

**SUGGESTED MAP** *OS Explorer OL 22 New Forest*

**START / FINISH** *Grid reference: SU 113184*

**DOG FRIENDLINESS** *Off lead in woodland, but keep under close control on farmland*

**PARKING** *Rockbourne village hall car park*

**PUBLIC TOILETS** *None en route*

Pevsner claims the village street in Rockbourne is one of the prettiest in Hampshire. This is certainly true, for the long, gently winding street in this peaceful and sheltered village, tucked in rolling downland on the borders with Wiltshire and Dorset, is lined with Tudor and Georgian houses and splendid thatched and timber-framed cottages.

By far the oldest known homestead is the Roman Villa, discovered south of the village by a farmer in 1942. He unearthed oyster shells and tiles and the significance of the find was recognised by local antiquarian A T Morley Hewitt, whose first excavation hole revealed a mosaic floor. In 1956, after Morley Hewitt had bought the land, a full-scale excavation began, and it was realised that the Rockbourne site was to be one of the most interesting Roman villa complexes to be discovered in the country.

## Roman Legacy

The Romans invaded Britain in AD 43 and quickly established roads, forts and towns. In the countryside, notably in southern England where the soils were fertile, they established prosperous farm estates with a villa at the centre. Villa architecture changed over the 400 years of Roman occupation. Simple circular houses were modified with the addition of wings, corridors, verandahs and courtyards, and housed heated bath suites and various farming activities.

Excavations at Rockbourne identified over 70 rooms, including the pre-Roman circular hut and elaborate bathhouses with underfloor heating. A treasure trove of Roman remains were also uncovered, in particular mosaics with geometric patterning, hoards of coins, elaborate ironwork, intricate jewellery, and shards of pottery with graffiti ranging from a simple symbol to a string of letters. Morley Hewitt's detailed study of the site has revealed much about the everyday life of the Roman Britons at Rockbourne. Sadly, the excavations have been filled in for their own protection, but you can see the outlines of the rooms and buildings marked out in the grass, the hypocaust heating systems and some mosaics.

The walk takes in the neighbouring village of Whitsbury, where foundations of a Roman building, containing a hypocaust and New Forest pottery of the 2nd and 3rd century AD, were found in a field between the church and Glebe House. There is also evidence of even earlier habitation in the village. At the northern end of the village, by Whitsbury Stud, is a fine example of a fortified Iron Age camp.

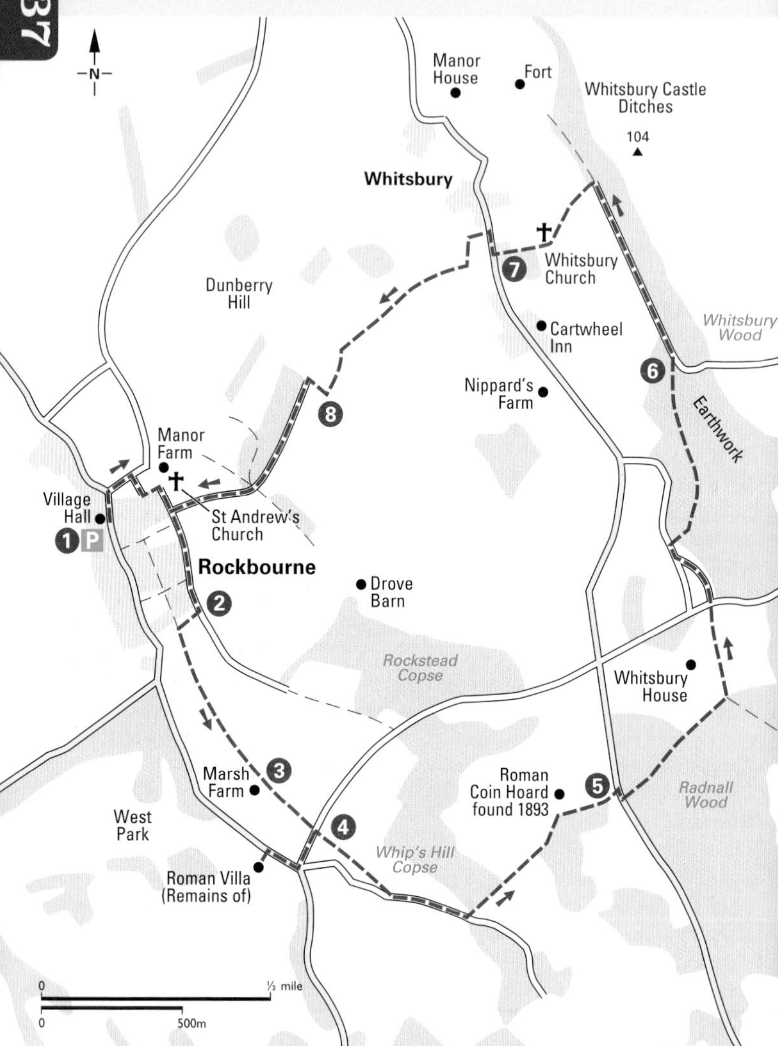


## WALK 37 DIRECTIONS

❶ Turn left out of the village hall car park and shortly take the lane right towards Manor Farm. Turn right, signed to the church, and cross the gravel drive to a stepped path to St Andrew's Church. Continue along the right-hand edge of the churchyard to reach a junction of paths. Keep straight on behind houses, ignoring three paths right, then cross a stile and turn immediately right to go through a gate.

❷ Follow the field-edge down to a junction of paths. Turn left and cross a stile to a gate, then cross a stile, go through a gate and along the field-edge. In the far corner of the field, zig-zag right and left over a stile and keep along the edge of a meadow to a stile. Pass in front of a thatched cottage to reach a gate and track, opposite Marsh Farm.

❸ Bear left, then right through a gate and continue along the right-hand field-edge to a gate. Continue to another gate, then turn left along the field-edge, passing through a gate to reach a stile and lane. To visit the Roman Villa, turn right to a T-junction, and turn right, then left to the entrance. Retrace your steps.

❹ Take the track opposite. Enter a copse, then at a junction of tracks, take the arrowed path left up a steep bank into a field. Follow the path parallel to the field-edge to reach a stile at the corner of a wood. Cross a track, and continue downhill inside the woodland edge to a lane.

❺ Turn right, then left along a bridleway, and gently climb through Radnall Wood. At a junction bear left (follow the blue arrow) and pass behind Whitsbury House to a lane. Turn left, then right along a track between properties to a lane. Turn right, then bear off right (by a fingerpost) along the bridleway through Whitsbury Wood.

❻ At a junction with a track, bear left and walk beside paddocks to a bungalow. Turn left along a track between paddocks towards Whitsbury church. Turn left at the T-junction and shortly enter the churchyard. Go through the gate opposite the church door and descend to the lane.

❼ Turn left for the Cartwheel Inn, otherwise turn right, then left along a farm drive and keep ahead, bearing left, then right between paddocks, uphill to a gate. Turn left along the field-edge, then head across the field to a track.

❽ Turn right and follow the track left to a junction of tracks. Go through the gate opposite and then walk back to Rockbourne church. Retrace your steps back to the village hall.

**WHILE YOU'RE THERE**

Visit the museum at the Roman Villa, which displays many of the artefacts, explains its development, and describes what life would have been like on this large Roman farm.

**WHAT TO LOOK FOR**

Interesting memorials to the Coote family, who lived at West Park to the south of the village can be seen in St Andrew's Church, Rockbourne. Lieutenant-General Sir Eyre Coote was the most famous, distinguishing himself as one of Clive of India's officers at the Battle of Plassey, in Bengal, in 1757. He is buried in the church and a 100ft (30m) monument was erected in West Park by the East India Company in 1828 to commemorate him.

**WHERE TO EAT AND DRINK**

The Rose & Thistle in Rockbourne is a thatched 17th-century building with an unspoilt interior. In Whitsbury, the Cartwheel is noted for its real ales, home-cooked food and peaceful garden.

# A Walk in Historic Breamore

*Exploring a classic estate village, the Avon Valley and its glorious surrounding downland.*

**DISTANCE** *6.25 miles (10.1km)* **MINIMUM TIME** *3hrs*
**ASCENT/GRADIENT** *315ft (96m)* ▲▲▲ **LEVEL OF DIFFICULTY** +++
**PATHS** *Field paths, water-meadows, woodland trails, 9 stiles*
**LANDSCAPE** *River valley and woodland on New Forest fringe*
**SUGGESTED MAP** *OS Explorer OL 22 New Forest, OS Explorer 130 Salisbury & Stonehenge*
**START / FINISH** *Grid reference: SU 151187 (on Explorer OL 22)*
**DOG FRIENDLINESS** *Under control at all times*
**PARKING** *Car park near Breamore House and Countryside Museum*
**PUBLIC TOILETS** *Opposite Countryside Museum (when the house is open)*

Breamore, pronounced 'Bremmer', is a truly ancient village. Stretching across the lush water-meadows and up the western chalk slopes of the Avon Valley, it is one of Hampshire's most impressive villages. Knots of 17th-century brick cottages and farmhouses, mostly thatched and timber-framed, are dotted around a large boggy common and close to Breamore's centrepiece, the fine Elizabethan manor house.

### Bloody Battle

The main village attractions are the manor, the Saxon church and Countryside Museum. Walk 39 climbs Breamore Down to the mystical Mizmaze and a prehistoric long barrow. Breamore's early history is encountered on the longer walk. As you venture across the water-meadows near South Charford Farm, you are on the site of the Battle of Charford (or Cerdicsford). Here, in AD 519, a bloody battle was fought between the native Britons from Old Sarum, and the Saxons, led by Cerdica. The Saxons won the day, slaying 5,000 Britons, the victory, arguably, leading to the creation of the Saxon Kingdom of Wessex.

The Church of St Mary, close to Breamore House, is a rare Saxon survivor having been built about AD 980. Despite later alterations, including a Norman porch and a 14th-century chancel, it still preserves much of the Saxon fabric, notably the extensive use of flints and some Roman bricks in its construction, small double-splayed windows, an Anglo-Saxon inscription, and a magnificent Saxon stone rood above the nave doorway. There's so much of interest here, so pick up a copy of the guide book before you explore. The pre-Reformation church was closely linked with Breamore Priory (1130–1536). The site can be seen beside the Avon just north of Breamore Mill. Following the Dissolution of the priory, a manor was built in 1583 by Queen Elizabeth's Treasurer, William Doddington. In warm red brick in the classic Elizabethan 'E' shape, it was purchased in the 18th century by Sir Edward Hulse, King George II's physician, and has remained the Hulse family home ever since.

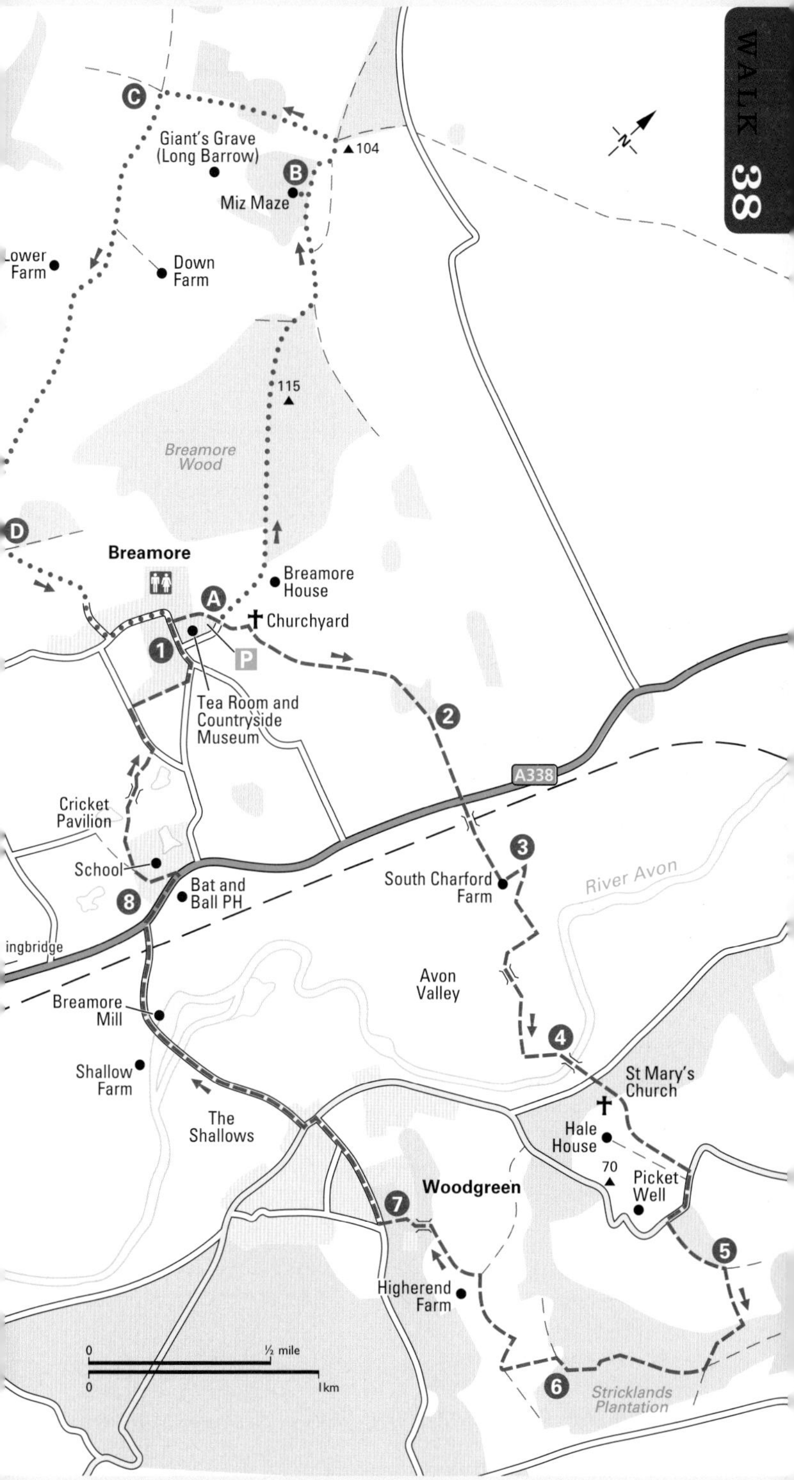

C
Giant's Grave (Long Barrow)
▲104
B
Miz Maze
Lower Farm
Down Farm
115
Breamore Wood
D
Breamore
A
Breamore House
Churchyard
1
P
Tea Room and Countryside Museum
2
A338
Cricket Pavilion
School
8
Bat and Ball PH
3
South Charford Farm
River Avon
ingbridge
Avon Valley
Breamore Mill
4
Shallow Farm
St Mary's Church
The Shallows
Hale House
70
Picket Well
Woodgreen
7
5
Higherend Farm
0 ½ mile
0 1km
6
Stricklands Plantation

## WALK 38 DIRECTIONS

1 Walk past the tea room and Countryside Museum and turn right beside the parkland wall. Cross the drive to Breamore House and walk to the church. Bear right then left through the churchyard to a gate. Head across pasture, cross a stile and bear half left to a stile. Keep to the left-hand field-edge to a gate and then turn right to walk through a copse to a stile.

2 Head straight across two fields, via stiles, and then cross the busy A338 (take care here). Cross a footbridge and stile beyond the lay-by, and walk across the field to some kissing gates. Maintain direction and follow the path through South Charford Farm.

3 Turn right along a track, follow it left (arrow on gate post), then right and left across the valley. Bear off left across an old sluice and cross the meadow beside a stream (it can be wet and boggy here) then cross the stile in the field corner on your left. Cross two sluice gates and several small footbridges, walking parallel with the River Avon to reach a gate and stile.

4 Cross the Avon and the lane, then climb the steep path to St Mary's Church. Keep to the path uphill, soon to run parallel with the drive to Hale House. Turn right at the lane, then left along a lane beside Garden Cottage.

5 At the end of the lane, fork right down a track and walk in front of Hemmick Court. Head downhill, then climb through woodland on a rhododendron-lined path. At a crossing of bridleways, turn right and proceed through Stricklands Plantation. Pass beneath an electricity pylon and soon descend to reach a junction of tracks.

6 Turn left and follow a drive to a T-junction of tracks. Turn right and gradually descend to a drive. Turn left, cross a stile to the right of a gate and head across pasture to a stile. Keep right along the field-edge to a gate and bear left downhill through woodland to a footbridge. Ascend between houses to a gravel track. Turn right, then left at the junction to the lane in Woodgreen.

7 Turn right downhill, pass the Horse and Groom, and follow the lane signed to Breamore. Cross the Avon Valley, passing Breamore Mill, to the A338. Turn right, pass the Bat and Ball and immediately cross the road to follow a lane left. Pass behind the school to join a track beside common land.

8 Bear off right on to the common, following the right-hand path towards a thatched cricket pavilion. Follow the path to the right of the cricket field, then turn left along a path to a footbridge and gravel drive. Bear right to a lane, opposite Orchard Cottage. Turn left and take the footpath right across a field to a lane. Turn left, then left again at the T-junction back to the car park.

**WHILE YOU'RE THERE**

Do not miss the Countryside Museum as it provides a fascinating insight into the days when a village was self-sufficient. You can see re-creations of village buildings and workshops, including a farm worker's cottage and a dairy, and view a vast collection of agricultural machinery and tractors.

# Breamore and the Miz Maze

*A shorter loop from the church in Breamore leads to the peculiar Miz Maze.*

**See map and information panel for Walk 38**



DISTANCE *4 miles (6.4km)* MINIMUM TIME *2hrs*

ASCENT/GRADIENT *279ft (85m)* ▲▲▲ LEVEL OF DIFFICULTY +++

## WALK 39 DIRECTIONS (Walk 38 option)

After visiting Breamore church walk back through the churchyard and take the bridleway on your right, walking between the gate pillars up the drive towards Breamore House (Point Ⓐ)

Pass the house and keep ahead, leaving the stables on your right as you ascend the track into Breamore Wood. Between 1239 and the 15th century this was a deer park, used for hunting by the Lords of the Manor. Keep to the main path as it curves right, then left (by a fingerpost) on leaving the trees. Bear left at a fork on the edge of rough grassland and keep ahead along a permissive path as far as a sign to the 'Miz Maze') Point Ⓑ.

Turn left into the dense hilltop yew grove to find the turf-cut Miz Maze. Legends about its origins abound, one associating it with monks from Breamore Priory, who had to crawl around the maze on their hands and knees as a penance. The circular maze is about 85ft (26m) in diameter and formed of 11 concentric rings.

At Point Ⓑ Leave the copse, turn left along the grassy swathe back down to the bridleway, and turn left. After 100yds (91m), turn left over a waymarked stile beside a gate and walk down the left-hand field-edge. Keep ahead as the path joins a track through woodland and continue past a metal barn, now walking along the woodland edge and down the side of the next field to a stile at Point Ⓒ.

Turn left on to the bridleway, which soon merges with a gravelled track. Pass a gate and keep ahead past the turning to Down Farm on your left. Continue past Lower Farm on your right, until you reach a metalled lane at Point Ⓓ.

Turn left here on to a bridleway, then fork immediately right on to a signposted path, heading diagonally across a field. Crest the brow of the hill and continue towards a thatched cottage, then cross a stile and turn right on to a metalled lane. Turn left at the bottom and follow the lane back to the car park.

### WHERE TO EAT AND DRINK

Light lunches and afternoon tea are served at the Tea Room from noon (Easter–September when the house is open). On the longer loop, call in at the Horse and Groom at Woodgreen or the Bat and Ball in Breamore.

WALK 40

# Keyhaven's Solent Shore

*A walk on the Solent Way and the wildlife-rich salt marsh west of Lymington.*

**DISTANCE** *5 miles (8km)* **MINIMUM TIME** *2hrs 30min*
**ASCENT/GRADIENT** *Negligible* ▲▲▲ **LEVEL OF DIFFICULTY** +++
**PATHS** *Sea wall path, tracks and short stretch of roade*
**LANDSCAPE** *Salt and freshwater marshland*
**SUGGESTED MAP** *OS Explorer OL 22 New Forest*
**START / FINISH** *Grid reference: SZ 306914*
**DOG FRIENDLINESS** *Off lead along sea wall path*
**PARKING** *Free parking by harbour wall or pay-and-display car park*
**PUBLIC TOILETS** *Keyhaven*

## WALK 40 DIRECTIONS

Between Hurst Spit at the western end of the Solent and the ancient town of Lymington lies a huge expanse of salt and freshwater marshes and mudflats, a breezy, watery landscape that's more reminiscent perhaps of East Anglia than Hampshire. The area is a birder's paradise, the marshes, lagoons and ponds attracting rare and interesting species, especially in the winter. So take your binoculars with you on this walk. From your vantage point on the sea wall you can scan the saltings and pools and see a wide range of waders and wildfowl. Guaranteed sightings will include a heron loping lazily across a lagoon, the curlew probing the mud with its long, down-curved bill, shelduck dabbling in the shallows, and soaring skylarks singing high above the reedbeds. Walk this way in winter and you should see huge flocks of black-necked brent geese feeding on the eelgrass, long-tailed ducks, greenshanks and, out on the Solent, goldeneye and common scoter. The elegant common and sandwich terns, which breed on Hurst Spit, can be seen overhead during the summer months and, if you're lucky, you may spot one of the rarer passage migrants, perhaps ruff, curlew sandpiper or little stint.

**WHERE TO EAT AND DRINK**

The 16th-century Chequers Inn, formerly the local salt exchange, in Pennington has a pleasant, sheltered terrace and garden, and offers a good snack menu and more imaginative dishes. The Gun Inn at Keyhaven is ideally placed for post-walk refreshment.

**WHAT TO LOOK OUT FOR**

Next door to the Gun in Keyhaven stands Hawkers Cottage, built by the famous wildfowler Peter Hawker in the early 19th century. He kept a diary detailing 50 years of hunting on the marshes.

Leave the car park and follow the Solent Way along the harbour wall heading east. Turn right through a gate beyond the parking area. Remain on the good shingle path close to the foreshore, then along the sea wall, with fine views across the Solent to Tennyson Down and Yarmouth on the Isle of Wight. Inland views take in the wildlife rich Keyhaven Marshes.

The area has not always been a refuge for wildlife. Between the 12th and 19th centuries salt extraction was a flourishing industry along this stretch of coastline. At one time there were 13 saltworks on Keyhaven and Pennington marshes. Sea water was impounded in shallow tidal ponds, or 'salterns', each about 20ft (6m) square, and left to evaporate. Once it had formed a strong brine, it was pumped by wind pump into boiling houses with coal-fired furnaces, where the water was boiled until salt crystals were left. Lymington salt was highly regarded and by the 18th century supplied much of southern England and was even exported to America. In 1800 4,000 tons were produced but when new railways brought in cheaper rock salt from Cheshire the industry declined. You can still see the remains of the old salt pans, square enclosures with low mud walls, from the sea wall.

Ignore all paths inland, your sea wall path skirting Oxey Marsh, with distant views of Lymington Marina, before heading west beside a channel to an old sluice gate. Keep ahead down four steps; then, after 120 yards (110m), turn right through a gate and head towards a house on a narrow path beside the creek. The two brick buildings you can see across the creek are old salt boiling houses. Shallow-draught lighters brought coal up the creek, known as Moses Dock, for the furnaces and returned loaded with salt.

Just before a squeeze stile, bear left and continue to a lane. Turn right here to visit the Chequers Inn. The Chequers' existence is closely linked with the salt industry. As well as being well-placed to serve the thirsty salt workers on their way home, it was where the outgoing salt was checked for tax purposes, hence its name.

Retrace your steps and keep to the lane to its end by Oxey Farm House. Keep ahead along the footpath to another lane and turn left. Follow it round a sharp right bend and walk beside Pennington Marshes. Where the lane ends, go ahead by a gate, signposted 'Cycle path to Keyhaven', and follow the track through the old saltings and beside Keyhaven Marshes to the harbour wall in Keyhaven.

**WHILE YOU'RE THERE**

Visit Hurst Castle. Between April and October, take the ferry or walk along the pebble beach to Henry VIII's fortress. Completed in 1544 to defend the Solent's western entrance, it was used to imprison Charles I in 1648 and housed coastal gun batteries and searchlights during the Second World War.

WALK 41

# A Forest Walk from Fritham

*A peaceful New Forest hamlet reveals its explosive history*

**DISTANCE** *5.5 miles (8.8km)* **MINIMUM TIME** *3hrs*

**ASCENT/GRADIENT** *328ft (100m)* ▲▲▲ **LEVEL OF DIFFICULTY** +++

**PATHS** *Gravel forest tracks, heathland and woodland paths*

**LANDSCAPE** *Ancient woodland and open heathland*

**SUGGESTED MAP** *OS Explorer OL 22 New Forest*

**START / FINISH** *Grid reference: SU 230141*

**DOG FRIENDLINESS** *Keep dogs under control at all times*

**PARKING** *Forestry Commission car park beyond Royal Oak*

**PUBLIC TOILETS** *None en route*

Fritham is an unspoilt commoning community nestling in a remote and peaceful enclave of pasture within the boundaries of the New Forest National Park. A scattering of cottages and farms, a chapel and a charming thatched pub are all that line the winding dead-end lane that leads straight on to the gorse and heather covered Fritham Plain. Many of the old cottages in the village have Forest Rights, which entitle the owners or tenants to graze cattle, horses and donkeys on the open forest, and to collect turf and wood for fuel. Pannage or mast rights also allow pigs to forage for acorns and beech masts in autumn to prevent the ponies from eating too many. These rights and the traditional commoners' way of life have existed for over 900 years. Here, on the forest fringe, you are likely to see domestic livestock, including enormous pigs, wandering, foraging and mixing with the New Forest ponies.

## A Shattered Peace

Fritham has not always been an idyllic rural scene. Its peace was shattered in 1865 when a German, Eduard Schultze, opened a gunpowder factory in an isolated glade beside the tree fringed Eyeworth Pond or Irons Well. Fritham's remote setting and the ready availability of charcoal, the main constituent of black gunpowder, made it an ideal location. Tracks from the village were strengthened to take the huge carts and the river was dammed to provide water power for the mills. As demand for smokeless sporting gunpowder increased, so the factory grew, eventually employing over 100 people from as far afield as Fordingbridge. After supplying gunpowder during the First World War, the factory was sold in 1923 and the operation was moved to Scotland.

Things went quiet for time – but, early in the Second World War, 4,000 acres (1,620ha) of nearby heathland were enclosed to create the Ashley Walk bombing range. Within its 9-mile (14.5km) perimeter fence, the site was a maze of natural and man-made targets that included bunkers, trenches and steel plates, as well as two massive concrete walls at Cockley Plain and Leaden Hall.

The range was the testing ground for a wide variety of military hardware, including the largest bomb ever to be dropped in England – the 22,000-lb 'Grand Slam' designed by Sir Barnes Wallis. Another of his creations, the famous 'Dam Buster' bouncing bomb, was also tested here. During the mid-1970s, one of these bombs was reconstructed out of sections salvaged from Ashley Walk, and presented to the RAF's 617 'Dam Buster' Squadron. Sir Barnes Wallis himself attended the ceremony, which was held at Middle Wallop air base, near Andover.

Over 400 craters were counted on aerial photos taken after the range closed in 1946. Now, more than 60 years later, the small brick observation shelter that you'll see near Ashley Cross is the only remaining building left standing from this time.

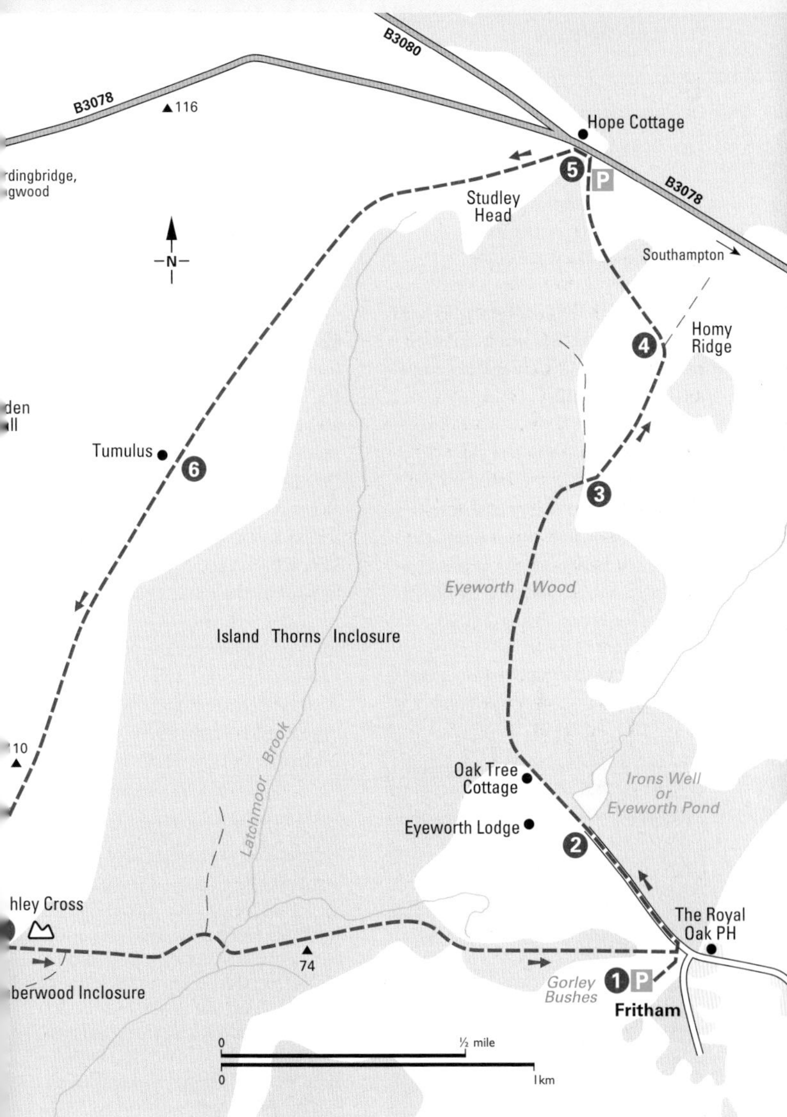

## WALK 41 DIRECTIONS

❶ Turn left out of the car park and head downhill along the road.

❷ Keep ahead at the foot of the hill, leaving Eyeworth Pond on your right, and follow the short gravel track to a low wooden barrier at Oak Tree Cottage. Leave the barrier on your left, take the narrow path that heads north into Eyeworth Wood, and follow it for 0.5 mile (800m).

❸ At length, the path leads on to a tree-studded heath, with far- reaching views. Continue for a further 550yds (503m) across Homy Ridge, as far as a stocky Scots pine tree at the edge of a small wood on your right.

❹ The path divides here. Take the left-hand fork, and walk through the shallow valley to the car park at Telegraph Hill.

❺ Turn left beside the B3078 for 20yds (18m), before turning left again on to the gravel track directly opposite Hope Cottage. The track bears left soon after passing a small, seasonal pond at Studley Head. After 250yds (229m), the path dives briefly beneath holly and oak trees before breaking back out on to the heath.

❻ Continue past a deep pool on your right, just a few paces beyond the low mound of a tumulus. Follow the track south towards Amberwood Inclosure, ignoring the path that branches off to your right near Ashley Bottom. A little further on, look for the small brick shelter located on your right.

❼ Turn left at a waymarked junction with the cycle track on the edge of Amberwood Inclosure, and dive steeply down the well-made gravel track into the woods. Ignore all turnings, and follow the waymarked route through the forest and over the Latchmoor Brook. The trees gradually drop behind as the cycle track winds its way up through Gorley Bushes, and there are glimpses of Eyeworth Lodge away to your left. A steady climb brings you to the green at Fritham. Turn right to return to the car park.

### WHAT TO LOOK FOR

Note the metal postbox by the car park entrance. Placed here pre-1900, it saved the postman his journey to the gunpowder factory and surrounding cottages. Look out too for deer. The New Forest owes its existence to deer as it was originally established by William the Conqueror in 1079 as a royal hunting ground. The fallow deer you are likely to see on the walk are directly descended from the beasts of the chase 900 years ago. The heather and gorse are also home to one of Britain's rarest heathland birds, the Dartford warbler.

### WHILE YOU'RE THERE

Visit the Rufus Stone between Brook and the A31. Erected in 1841, it is said to mark the spot where William II, the Conqueror's son, was killed accidentally while out hunting in 1100.

### WHERE TO EAT AND DRINK

With its thatch, scrubbed pine tables and relaxed, informal garden, The Royal Oak is the perfect retreat before or after your walk. Ringwood tops the list of local ales, and the down-to-earth menu includes home-made pies, local sausages and winter soups, as well as ploughman's lunches. The pub is open all day at weekends, and during school holidays.

# Godshill to Appuldurcombe

*Traverse unspoilt downland from Godshill to the ruins of a Palladian mansion.*

**DISTANCE** *4.5 miles (7.2km)* **MINIMUM TIME** *2hrs*
**ASCENT/GRADIENT** *639ft (195m)* ▲▲▲ **LEVEL OF DIFFICULTY** +++
**PATHS** *Downland, woodland paths, tracks, metalled drive, 2 stiles*
**LANDSCAPE** *Farmland, woodland, and open downland*
**SUGGESTED MAP** *OS Explorer OL 29 Isle of Wight*
**START / FINISH** *Grid reference: SZ 530817*
**DOG FRIENDLINESS** *Dogs must be kept on lead in places*
**PARKING** *Free car park in Godshill, opposite The Griffin*
**PUBLIC TOILETS** *Godshill, opposite The Griffin*

With its village street lined with pretty thatched cottages, flower-filled gardens, wishing wells, souvenir shops, and tea gardens, Godshill, at its most visible, is the tourist 'honey-pot' on the island. It is best explored out of season, when the coaches and crowds have gone, and its period buildings and magnificent church can be better appreciated. Godshill is also located in the heart of an unspoilt landscape and perfect walking country, making it a useful starting point for several exhilarating downland rambles.

## Family Tie

The history of Godshill is closely tied to the Worsley family, builders of the Palladian-style mansion of Appuldurcombe in the neighbouring village of Wroxall and the focus of this walk. Several of the buildings in the village were built by various owners of Appuldurcombe and their fine memorials can be seen in the church. Your walk quickly escapes Godshill and the throng of summer visitors, steadily climbing through woods and farmland to the top of Stenbury Down, where you can catch your breath and take in the far-reaching island views, from Tennyson Down in the west to Culver Cliff in the east. From these lofty heights, you quickly descend towards Wroxall to reach the magnificent ruins of Appuldurcombe House.

Cradled in a sheltered and secluded natural amphitheatre beneath high downland slopes, Appuldurcombe, the great house of Wroxall, began as a priory in 1100. It later became a convent and then the home of the Leigh family in 1498. The connection with the illustrious Worsleys began when the Leighs' daughter Anne married Sir James Worsley, the richest man in Wight, who obtained a new lease. Following the Dissolution of the Monasteries, the Worsley's gained outright possession of the property, pulled down the old Tudor house and built a fine mansion with a pillared front towards the end of the 18th century. They also employed 'Capability' Brown to landscape the immediate surroundings of the house. It was, by far, the grandest house on the island until Queen Victoria built Osborne House. After 300 years as the home of the Worsley family, it was sold in 1854 and in succeeding years became a school, the home of Benedictine monks, and a temporary base for troops during World War One. Already damaged and decaying, it was finally reduced to a ruined shell in 1943, courtesy of a stray German land mine.

What you see today has been achieved by English Heritage and its predecessors, who since 1952 have repaired and restored the dramatic shell of the building, finally re-roofing and replacing windows in the Great Hall, Drawing Room and Dining Parlour in 1986. Visitors can wander through the eerily empty rooms, admire the splendid east front and stroll through the ornamental gardens and 11 acres (4.5ha) of grounds.

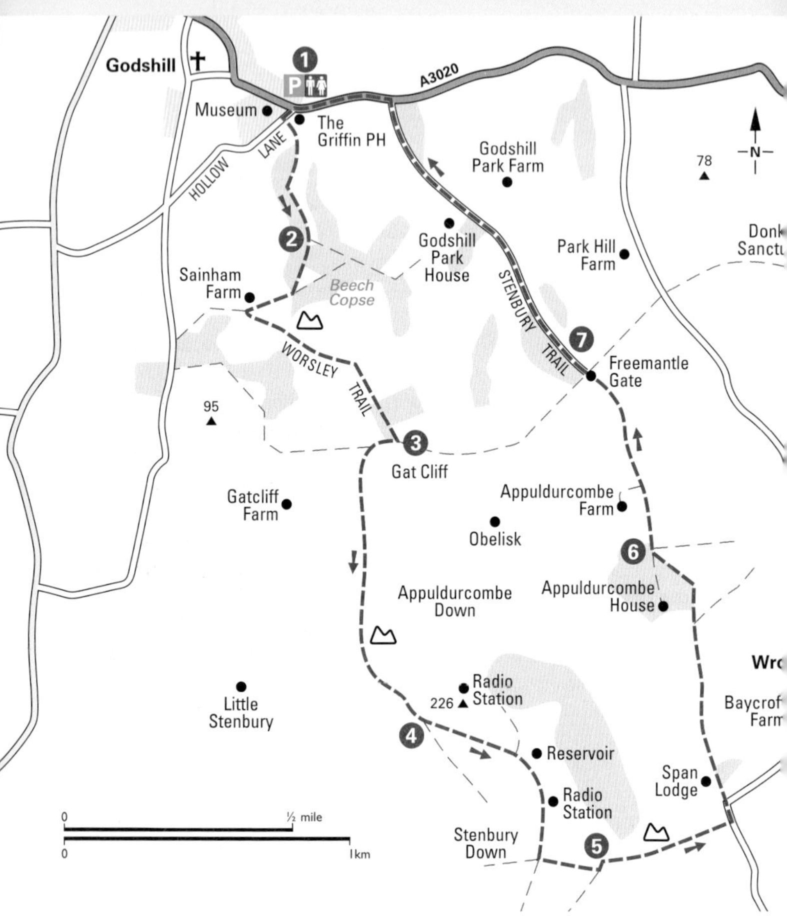


## WALK 42 DIRECTIONS

1 From the car park in Godshill, cross the road and walk down Hollow Lane beside the Griffin Inn. Just before Godshill Cherry Orchard, take the footpath left, signed to Beech Copse. Keep to the right of the pub garden and continue gently uphill through the valley to a kissing gate on the edge of Beech Copse.

2 Just beyond, at a fork, bear right uphill through trees to a junction of paths by a gate. Turn right through the gate and walk towards Sainham Farm. Keep left of the farm to a gate and turn left uphill (Worsley Trail), signed to

Stenbury Down. Steadily climb this fenced track, passing two large metal gates to enter a copse.

3 At a junction of paths below Gat Cliff, take bridleway GL49 right through a gate beside a fingerpost, signed 'Stenbury Down'. Shortly, disregard footpath right and keep to the bridleway as it veers left and climbs to a gate. Skirting around the base of Gat Cliff and then Appuldurcombe Down, the path follows field-edges before climbing steeply beside a stone wall to a gate and open grassland on the top of Stenbury Down.

4 Keep left beside the hedge to a gate and, in a few paces, bear right along the track towards a radio station. Pass to the left of the building; then, just before reaching a stile and footpath on the right, turn left through a waymarked gate along the field-edge. Head downhill, then at the field boundary, bear left to descend steps to a metalled track.

5 Turn left and steeply descend to a T-junction. Turn left then, where the lane curves right, keep ahead to pass Span Lodge and a large barn to a gate. Keep ahead between fields to a stile. Keep to the left-hand field-edge in front of Appuldurcombe House, ignoring the waymarked path right, to a stile by the entrance to the house.

6 Take the footpath to the left of the car park, signed 'Godshill'. Walk along the drive to Appuldurcombe Farm then, where it curves left, keep straight ahead through two gateways (with stiles to the left) and soon pass through Freemantle Gate on the edge of Godshill Park.

7 Proceed downhill towards Godshill Park Farm. Ignore paths right and left, pass in front of Godshill Park House and join the metalled drive that leads to the A3020. Cross over and turn left along the pavement back to the car park.

### WHILE YOU'RE THERE

Visit the Isle of Wight Natural History Centre in Godshill. Housed in a 17th-century cottage, you can marvel at a collection of some 40,000 seashells and corals, together with minerals, precious and semi-precious stones, the largest collection of its kind in Southern England. Buy a joint ticket at Appuldurcombe House and visit the Owl and Falconry Centre to see aviaries with birds of prey and owls from around the world, and regular flying displays.

### WHERE TO EAT AND DRINK

There's a good range of pubs, cafés and tea rooms in Godshill, notably the Cask and Taverners pub and the Willow Tree Tea Gardens. The welcome Aviary Café is at the Owl and Falconry Centre at Appuldurcombe House (admission charge).

### WHAT TO LOOK OUT FOR

Escape the crowds and the knick-knack shops in Godshill and make for All Saints Church, a large, medieval parish church on a hill surrounded by pretty thatched cottages. Look for the late 15th-century wall painting of Christ crucified (the Lily Cross), a painting which may be by Rubens, and the magnificent Tudor monuments to the Leigh and Worsley families.

# Downlands to Brighstone

*From the downland above Brighstone to the wild and beautiful shore.*

**DISTANCE** *8.25 miles (13.3km)* **MINIMUM TIME** *4hrs*
**ASCENT/GRADIENT** *941ft (287m)* ▲▲▲ **LEVEL OF DIFFICULTY** +++
**PATHS** *Field and clifftop paths, woodland tracks, 9 stiles*
**LANDSCAPE** *Farmland, chalk downland, woodland and coastal scenery*
**SUGGESTED MAP** *OS Explorer OL 29 Isle of Wight*
**START / FINISH** *Grid reference: SZ 385835*
**DOG FRIENDLINESS** *Off lead on Mottistone Down, otherwise keep under control*
**PARKING** *National Trust car park at Brook Chine*
**PUBLIC TOILETS** *Brighstone*

The heart of old Brighstone is undoubtedly one of the prettiest village scenes on the island, full of old-world charm with thatched golden-stone cottages, tea gardens and a fine Norman church. It lies tucked away under the downland ridge in the centre of the south-west coastal shelf, less than a mile (1.6km) from the coast, and the beautiful surrounding countryside is perfect for walking.

In fact, the varied nature of the landscape around the village is a microcosm of the island as a whole. Stroll south through the fields and you are on the wild and beautiful shore, with miles of sand and rock ledges. Puff your way north on to Brighstone Down, and you reach the largest area of forest on the island, dotted with Bronze Age and Neolithic burial mounds.

A sense of history pervades Brighstone, no more so following a visit to the tiny village museum. Here you will discover its notorious past. From the 13th century to the late 1800s, Brighstone was a noted smuggling village, with many of the locals involved in wrecking and contraband. Good money could be earned salvaging cargoes and timbers from ships wrecked along the coast, and it was common for local children to seek credit from the Brighstone shopkeeper by promising 'Mother will pay next shipwreck'. It was not until the 1860s that the first lifeboats were launched from Brighstone and Brook. Revd McCall aroused residents' consciences to Christian compassion for shipwrecked mariners, local benefactor Charles Seeley provided the finance, and reformed smuggler James Buckett, having served five years compulsory service in the navy as punishment for his crimes, became the first coxwain of the Brighstone boat.

Brighstone is also famous for the fact that three of its rectors were later appointed bishops. Thomas Ken was rector in 1667 and wrote the famous hymn 'Glory to thee, my God this night' before becoming Bishop of Bath and Wells. Samuel Wilberforce, son of the great anti-slavery campaigner William Wilberforce, was rector here for ten years (1830–40), founding the library and school, before being appointed Bishop of Winchester. Finally, in 1866, George Moberly arrived in the village, leaving three years later to become Bishop of Salisbury.

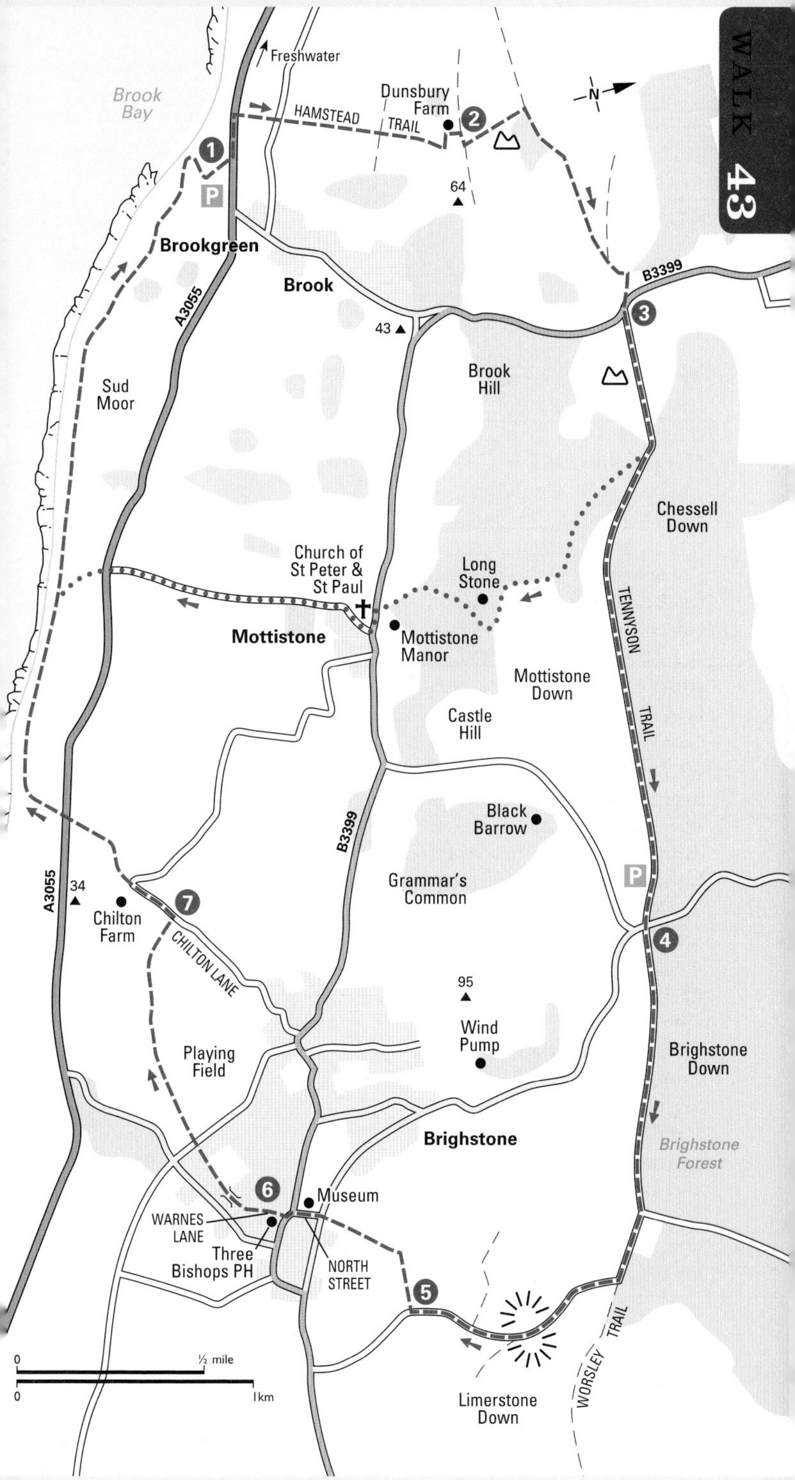

Freshwater
Brook Bay
HAMSTEAD TRAIL
Dunsbury Farm
N
1
2
64
P
Brookgreen
Brook
B3399
43
3
A3055
Sud Moor
Brook Hill
Chessell Down
Church of St Peter & St Paul
Long Stone
Mottistone
Mottistone Manor
TENNYSON TRAIL
Mottistone Down
Castle Hill
Black Barrow
B3399
P
A3055
34
Chilton Farm
7
Grammar's Common
CHILTON LANE
4
95
Wind Pump
Playing Field
Brighstone Down
Brighstone
Brighstone Forest
6
Museum
WARNES LANE
Three Bishops PH
NORTH STREET
5
WORSLEY TRAIL
½ mile
1km
Limerstone Down

## WALK 43 DIRECTIONS

❶ From the car park, turn left along the A3055 to a stile on the right, waymarked Hamstead Trail, and walk across the field to a track. Keep ahead beside cottages and maintain direction on reaching a crossing of tracks, heading uphill on a metalled track. Bear left then right around Dunsbury Farm to a T-junction.

❷ Turn right, then immediately left through a gate and ascend steeply between trees to a gate. Merge with a track at a junction and bear right. Go through a gate and continue to climb, shortly bearing right (marked by a blue byway sign) to follow the track downhill beside a line of electricity poles. Keep right at a chalk track, go through a gate and cross the B3399 to a gate and bridleway, signed to Carisbrooke.

❸ Climb steadily along the main Tennyson Trail across the downland to a gate on the top of Mottistone Down. Descend to the car park and turn right along the lane. In a few paces turn left along a stony track.

❹ Follow the Tennyson Trail uphill beside Brighstone Forest. At the second junction of paths (by a fingerpost), take the bridleway right through a gate and descend Limerstone Down on a gorse-edged path with superb views. Ignore turnings left and right; then, just beyond a stile, turn right on to a grassy bridleway for Brighstone.

❺ Head downhill through bracken and join a sandy path between trees to Brighstone. Cross the lane, walk along North Street, passing the village museum, to the B3399. Turn left, then right beside the Three Bishops pub into Warnes Lane.

❻ Keep left of the car park along a metalled path to a road. Turn right, then left with a waymarker and cross a footbridge. Keep to the left-hand edge of the playing field and to the rear of gardens to a lane. Cross straight over the lane and follow the fenced path to Chilton Lane.

❼ Turn left, pass Chilton Farm and keep ahead at the sharp right-hand bend along a track to the A3055. Pass through the car park opposite and follow the path to the coast. Turn right along the coast path and soon cross a stile on to National Trust land (Sud Moor). Keep to the coast path, crossing four stiles to reach Brookgreen. Bear right beside the Chine and cottages and turn left to a stile and the car park.

**WHAT TO LOOK FOR**

Mottistone Down is rich in wildlife. Look out for chalk-loving plants like rock roses, horseshoe vetch and the clustered bell flower that flourish here. There are 30 species of butterfly that feed on the flowers, including chalkhill blues and fritillaries.

**WHERE TO EAT AND DRINK**

The Three Bishops and a tea room in Brighstone, and a coffee shop in the Isle of Wight Pearl complex on the Walk 43. Afternoon teas are available in Mottistone Manor Garden.

# Past the Long Stone

*A shorter loop takes you past the Long Stone and over Mottistone Down.*

**See map and information panel for Walk 43**



DISTANCE *5 miles (8km)* MINIMUM TIME *2hrs 30min*

ASCENT/GRADIENT *626ft (191m)* ▲▲▲ LEVEL OF DIFFICULTY +++

## WALK 44 DIRECTIONS (Walk 43 option)

Having climbed steadily across downland from Point 3, go through the gate and in 60yds (55m) bear off right to follow the bridleway across rough heathland. Pass through a gate into woodland, and follow the path to a kissing gate. Turn left and follow the track to the Long Stone.

The Long Stone is a free-standing upright stone of local greensand beside which lies another large stone. They have been the subject of many mystical theories, but the true archaeological explanation is that they are the remains of a Stone Age burial chamber, or long barrow, located behind the stone. They were erected some 4,000 years ago and in Saxon times were used as a meeting place or 'moot', hence the origin of the name 'Mottistone'.

Turn right here and take the narrow path into the trees and undergrowth. Cross a track at a kissing gate and continue through the woods to the road by Mottistone Manor. The lower slopes of Mottistone Down are covered in old beech, oak and sycamore and you will find the path to the village lined with wild cherry trees and bluebells in spring.

Bear left, pass the church, and take the byway right opposite the Manor. With its pretty cottages, stone manor house and 13th-century church overlooking the green, Mottistone is very much the quintessential English village. You can admire the mullioned windows and ancient stone walls of the Elizabethan manor (not open to the public) from the beautiful hillside garden, which is noted for its colourful herbaceous borders and terraces planted with fruit trees. The Church of St Peter and St Paul is well worth a closer look. Here you can see a Jacobean pulpit and wood salvaged from the *Cedrine*, a ship wrecked on the beach in 1862, in the chancel roof. Local smuggling tales abound, including the story of a family table-tomb in the churchyard being used to hide barrels of brandy.

Follow the hedged track downhill to a gate and the main road. Cross the stile opposite and keep to the right-hand field-edge to a stile. Turn right at a third stile and re-join Walk 43 along the coast path, crossing four stiles back to Brookgreen. Bear right beside Brook Chine and cottages, then bear left to a stile and to return to the car park.

# Breezy Bembridge

*Follow the coastal path to Culver Cliff and visit the island's only windmill.*

**DISTANCE** *5 miles (8km)* **MINIMUM TIME** *2hrs 30min*

**ASCENT/GRADIENT** *410ft (125m)* ▲▲▲ **LEVEL OF DIFFICULTY** +++

**PATHS** *Coastal and field paths, some road, 3 stiles*

**LANDSCAPE** *Coastal cliffs and chalk downland*

**SUGGESTED MAP** *OS Explorer OL 29 Isle of Wight*

**START / FINISH** *Grid reference: SZ 657880*

**DOG FRIENDLINESS** *Keep dogs under control, can run free on Culver Down*

**PARKING** *Bembridge pay-and-display car park*

**PUBLIC TOILETS** *Beside car park and Bembridge Harbour*

## WALK 45 DIRECTIONS

Bembridge is almost a place apart on the island's most easterly headland. Formerly a rough fishing and smuggling hamlet, it was transformed by a few wealthy Victorians into a fashionable resort with hotels and holiday villas in their own grounds. Centred around its attractive and tranquil small harbour, dotted with colourful boats and popular with visiting yachtsmen, Bembridge remains an affluent resort village.

Walk to the sea wall, turn right and soon follow the coastal path inland. Cross the drive to the Bembridge Coast Hotel, the fenced path leading to a track. Turn left to a road, then turn right and take the second road (Beachfield Road) left. At the end, follow the coastal path right, pass in front of the coastguard station and keep left of the Crab and Lobster. Keep to the coast, passing steps down to the beach and the Cabin Café, to a junction of paths. Turn left, then bear right and pass through woodland. Soon skirt the grounds to Bembridge Environmental Field Study Centre before descending steps into woodland.

Pass in front of Whitecliff Bay Holiday Parks. Now turn right, then left, around the front of Nab Bars to a small tarmac area at the far corner of the buildings. Turn left here, along a narrow enclosed path leading to a lane.

Here, you may take the short, steep diversions to the Yarborough

Monument. Turn left past Glover's Farm and keep ahead over the stile when the lane bends right. Cross the field to a gate and second stile, then bear left up the steep track to the monument. Retrace your steps to the lane.

The monument on top of Culver Down is dedicated to Lord Yarborough who founded the Royal Yacht Club, the first of its kind, in 1815. It was later renamed The Royal Yacht Squadron and has its headquaters in Cowes. Algernon Swinburne, the great Victorian poet, who lived at Bonchurch, knew and loved Culver Down, often seeking inspiration here. He once climbed its precipitous cliff!

Otherwise, turn right and continue to a road junction. Turn right for 100yds (91m) and turn left along a narrow lane. At the B3395, opposite Bembridge Airport, cross over and turn right. Descend and take the bridleway left, signed to Bembridge Windmill. Continue through woodland, then follow the track uphill to the windmill.

Bembridge Windmill, built in 1700, is the last surviving windmill on the island. It is a fascinating piece of 17th-century industrial archaeology and you will find much of the original wooden machinery, including the sails, still intact. View various artefacts on three floors and savour the views from the top.

At the lane, bear left into Bembridge. In 0.5 mile (800m), take the footpath left, signed to the 'Point'. Descend and bear right, soon to join a track to the B3395 at Bembridge Harbour. Cross over into Pump Lane and follow the coastal path sign. Pass houses to a track and keep ahead on the coastal path to the junction with Swains Lane. The coastal path turns left here, then right along the beach to the car park.

This section is heavy going, so it's safer to keep ahead along Swains Lane to the junction with Lane End Road. Turn left for the short walk back to the car park.

### WHILE YOU'RE THERE

Visit the Shipwreck and Maritime Museum in Bembridge. Fascinating collections, spread over six galleries, illustrate the maritime history of the island, including artefacts recovered from shipwrecks, antique diving equipment, and Spanish 'pieces of eight'. On certain days you can enjoy a guided tour of the Lifeboat Station at the end of the long jetty by the start point car park.

### WHERE TO EAT AND DRINK

There are various cafés along the way, notably at Bembridge Harbour, by the Lifeboat Station and beside the beach close to Foreland. The pub on Culver Down has good views. The Pilot Boat Inn at Bembridge Harbour and the Crab and Lobster serve good fresh fish, the latter also having sea views.

### WHAT TO LOOK OUT FOR

From the top of Culver Down you have magnificent views over the south-east corner of the island, across Bembridge Harbour towards the Spithead Forts and Portsmouth. To the west the view takes in the whole sweep of Sandown Bay and inland along the ridge of chalk downland.

# Carisbrooke's Castle

*Explore a castle with strong royal associations and visit an isolated church.*

**DISTANCE** *6.5 miles (10.4km)* **MINIMUM TIME** *2hrs 30min*

**ASCENT/GRADIENT** *764ft (233m)* ▲▲▲ **LEVEL OF DIFFICULTY** +++

**PATHS** *Field and downland paths and tracks, some roads, 5 stiles*

**LANDSCAPE** *Farmland and open chalk downland*

**SUGGESTED MAP** *OS Explorer OL 29 Isle of Wight*

**START / FINISH** *Grid reference: SZ 489876*

**DOG FRIENDLINESS** *Keep dogs under control*

**PARKING** *Car park close to Carisbrooke Priory*

**PUBLIC TOILETS** *Carisbrooke Castle*

On a spur of chalk downland, 150ft (46m) above the village, the site of a Roman fort, Carisbrook Castle, a grand medieval ruin, commands a perfect military location, overlooking the Bowcombe Valley and the approaches to the heart of the island. You can walk the battlements, experience the majestic location and admire the countryside below, much of the view encompassing the walk ahead.

## Norman Strength

The castle is probably of Saxon origin, but it was the Normans who strengthened the site, building the stone walls, the gatehouse and the keep, on a mound within the walls. The outer bastions were built to guard against the 16th-century threat of Spanish invasion. It was said that 'He who held Carisbrooke, held the Isle of Wight.' For centuries the castle went hand-in-hand with the lordship of the island, before the Crown retained the lordship in the 16th century and appointed a Governor of the Island, a title that continues today. The Great Hall, which was the official residence of the Island Governor until 1944, now houses the Isle of Wight Museum. At Carisbrooke Castle Story in the gatehouse, you'll learn more about the two occasions when it experienced military action, and find many exhibits about the castle's most famous royal visitor, King Charles I. He sought refuge here during the Civil War in November 1647, but was imprisoned by the Governor until September 1648 before being taken to London for trial and execution. He made two unsuccessful attempts to escape – you can see the window where the King cut the bars before he was thwarted. His children, the future Charles II, Henry, Duke of Gloucester, and 14 year-old Elizabeth (who died of pneumonia) were also detained here in 1650.

Leaving the castle, you'll walk through the Bowcombe Valley, beside the Lukely Brook, to the isolated village of Gatcombe, nestling in a valley. Quarries here provided stone for the building of Carisbrooke Castle. Each stone, it is said, was passed along a human chain to the site 2 miles (3.2km) away. Take a little time to explore the 13th-century church before joining the Shepherds Trail back to Carisbrooke.

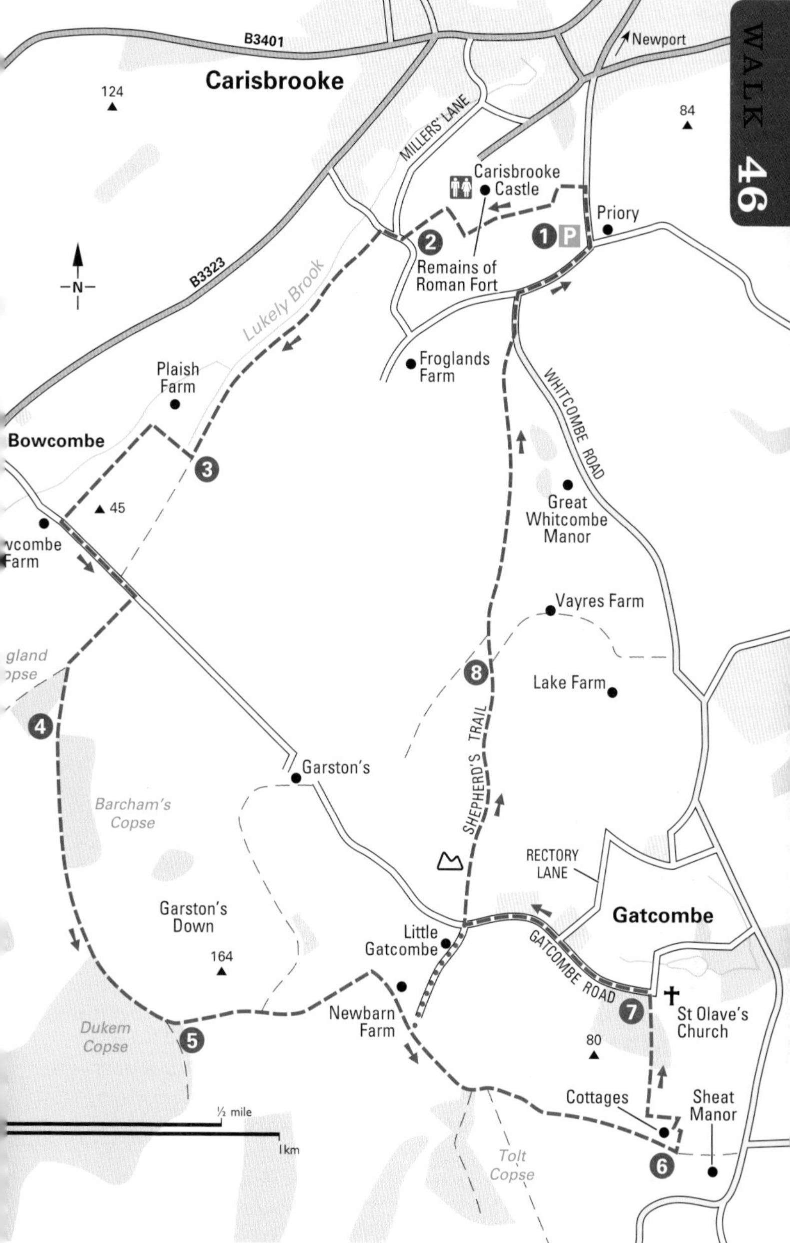


## WALK 46 DIRECTIONS

1 From the car park, and facing Carisbrooke Priory, turn left and walk along the road. Take the first left-hand footpath and veer left after a few steps, climbing gently through the trees. On reaching the magnificent ruins of Carisbrooke Castle, bear left and follow the path alongside the castle walls. Turn left on reaching the car park and follow the public footpath sign for Millers Lane.

2 Turn right on reaching the road, pass Millers Lane and walk to a stile and path on the left, signposted 'Bowcombe'. Cross the field to the next stile and keep going across the pastures, crossing several more stiles. Level with Plaish Farm, make for a stile and junction ahead.

3 Turn right here and follow the enclosed path, bending left after 150yds (137m). On reaching Bowcombe Farm, turn left and follow the sign for Gatcombe. Pass an unmarked footpath on the left, and continue on the track as it curves right, avoiding the track running straight ahead. Veer away left at the corner of Frogland Copse and follow the field-edge to a bridleway sign.

4 Bear right through the trees to a gate and continue ahead up the slope, skirting the field boundary. Keep ahead in the next field, passing through the gate and into Dukem Copse. Follow the track inside the woodland edge as far as the signposted turning towards Gatcombe on your left.

5 Go through a gate and continue along the field-edge. On reaching a path to Garstons, descend to the right and then swing left to a gate. Follow the bridleway for Gatcombe and turn right to Newbarn Farm. Bear right at the entrance and, at the lane, keep right along the bridleway. At the edge of Tolt Copse ignore the path right and bear left, soon to leave the Shepherd's Trail, keeping ahead along a bridleway continuing towards Sheat Manor.

**WHERE TO EAT AND DRINK**

Try the tea room at Carisbrooke Castle (open April–October) or at Little Gatcombe Farm in Gatcombe. There are two pubs in Carisbrooke.

6 Before the manor, at a junction of paths, turn left, following the path past cottages, then bear left again and keep to the winding path as it ascends to woodland. Proceed through the wood and descend to a lane beside St Olave's Church.

7 Turn left to walk along Gatcombe Road, pass Rectory Lane, then turn right at a crossing of ways, rejoining the Shepherd's Trail for Carisbrooke. Pass between properties and climb quite steeply through trees. Pass over a track, then go through a gate and follow the path round the left-hand field-edge.

**WHILE YOU'RE THERE**

Visit Carisbrooke Castle. Walk the battlements and savour the majestic view over the surrounding countryside, locate the two medieval wells, one with winding gear driven by a donkey, see the Carisbrooke Castle Story in the gatehouse and discover more about the history of the island in the Isle of Wight Museum in the Great Hall.

8 Go through another gate and keep beside the field boundary. Now the path becomes enclosed by a fence and hedge; ignore the bridleway to Vayres and Cox's Corner on your right, and continue past a sign for Carisbrooke and Whitcombe Road. Keep to the obvious path and eventually reach a junction. Walk ahead to the car park.

# The Peeping Pepperpot

*An invigorating walk around the island's most southerly point.*



**DISTANCE** *5.5 miles (8.8km)* **MINIMUM TIME** *2hrs*

**ASCENT/GRADIENT** *745ft (227m)* ▲▲▲ **LEVEL OF DIFFICULTY** +++

**PATHS** *Field paths, downland tracks, coast path, 8 stiles*

**LANDSCAPE** *Rolling downland and farmland, breezy cliff top*

**SUGGESTED MAP** *OS Explorer OL 29 Isle of Wight*

**START / FINISH** *Grid reference: SZ 490767*

**DOG FRIENDLINESS** *Keep dogs under control at all times*

**PARKING** *Free parking in viewpoint car park above Blackgang Chine*

**PUBLIC TOILETS** *Niton*

The viewpoint car park high above Blackgang Chine is the ideal starting point for this intriguing ramble around the island's most southerly point, an area steeped in tales about shipwrecks, smuggling and three lighthouses. Before you lies the broad sweep of Chale Bay and high upon St Catherine's Hill to your right is a curious octagonal tower, known locally as the 'Pepperpot'. For centuries Chale Bay, in particular the treacherous rocks around Atherfield Ledge, was notorious for shipwrecks and the subsequent looting of desirable cargoes. Violent storms and huge seas drove fully-rigged sailing ships crashing against the cliffs, once as many as 14 floundered in the 'Bay of Death' on one single night.

## Medieval Lighthouse

Your walk begins with a long, steady climb up St Catherine's Hill to the 'Pepperpot' and it is only here that you really realise its significance. It's all that remains of a medieval lighthouse or beacon and is, equally, a monument to the folly of Walter de Godeton. Its story begins with the wreck of a merchant ship, the *Ship of the Blessed Mary*, at Atherfield Ledge in 1313, while bound for England with a consignment of wine. The sailors escaped and sold the 174 casks of wine to the islanders, one of whom was Walter de Godeton who took 53 casks. As it belonged to a religious community in Normandy, it was considered an offence to receive the smuggled wine. Following a long trial, de Godeton was fined heavily and as an act of penance was ordered to build a pharos and oratory on the site of an earlier hermitage, so that a priest could tend the light and say prayers for those lost at sea.

The oratory has long since disappeared, but the lighthouse, operational until 1638, survives as Britain's only medieval lighthouse. Close by is another partially built lighthouse known as the 'Mustard Pot'. Begun in 1785 to rekindle the St Catherine's light, the project was abandoned due to cost and the realisation that its warning light would rarely be visible due to fog. It was not until the tragic loss of the *Clarendon* in 1836 that the present lighthouse at St Catherine's Point was built.

WALK 47

## BLACKGANG CHINE

At the end of the St Catherine's Down stands Hoy's Monument, a 72ft (22m) high column commemorating the visit of a Russian Tzar in 1814. The views from the ridge are spectacular and the walk culminates above the dramatic undercliff of St Catherine's Point.

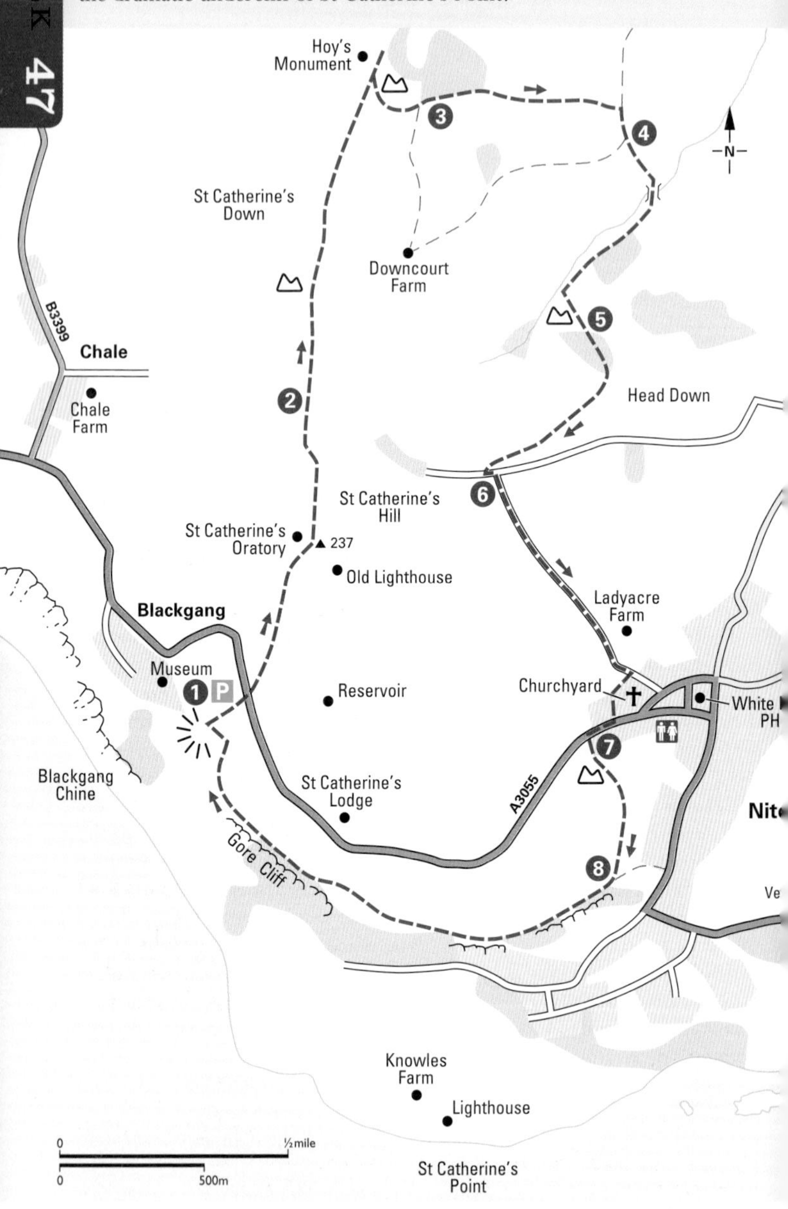


### WALK 47 DIRECTIONS

❶ From the car park, cross the road and climb steps to a gate. Bear left, signposted towards 'St Catherine's Oratory'. Pass a broken stile and steadily climb up the grassy downland to a stile. Walk up to the old lighthouse, known locally as the Pepperpot.

Ignore the stile by the trig point just beyond; then, keeping the fence on your right, continue downhill and bear left to a gate.

❷ Go through the gate and proceed ahead on the broad grassy swathe to Hoy's Monument. Return for 80yds (73m) and take the bridleway left. Descend steeply through trees and bear left with the main path downhill to a gate. Follow the bridleway left, then bear right along the driveway.

❸ Proceed ahead at a crossing of tracks (Downcourt Farm drive is to the right), heading downhill to a gate by a house. Walk along the right-hand field-edge to a gate and head downhill on a hedged path. At a T-junction, turn right and go through a gate, the path soon emerging into a field.

❹ Keep to the left-hand field-edge, beside an overgrown gully, and cross the first stile on the left. In a few paces, turn right, then take the path left just before another gate. Head through the trees, cross a concrete bridge and keep right. Gradually ascend a stony path, which is very wet in winter, and which bears left then steepens to reach a stile.

❺ Walk ahead, following the defined path uphill beside a hedge to two stiles in the field corner. Cross the right-hand stile and immediately turn right, down on to a path that heads diagonally uphill across the face of Head Down to a stile. Turn left to a stile and track.

❻ Turn left, then almost immediately right along a hedged bridleway. Head downhill, the path becoming metalled as it enters Niton. Just before the lane, bear right into the churchyard. (Turn left, then first right, for the White Lion). Keep left, exit the churchyard by a small gate and turn right alongside the A3055.

❼ Take the footpath beside the last house on the left and climb up steeply through trees to a stile. Walk ahead across grassland to a stile and follow the left-hand field-edge to a kissing gate.

❽ Turn right along the coastal path, through two kissing gates and soon emerge on to open cliff top. Remain on this narrow path close to the cliff edge for nearly a mile (1.6km) back to the car park.

### WHERE TO EAT AND DRINK

During the summer and at weekends you may find an ice cream van in the car park. The White Lion in Niton, once the haunt of smugglers, serves a varied menu and real ale. After the walk, retire to the Wight Mouse Inn in Chale.

### WHILE YOU'RE THERE

Visit St Andrew's Church in Chale. It has withstood more than five centuries of storms, and from the churchyard, there is a fine view of this wild stretch of coast. Among the many graves are those of sailors who died when the *Clarendon* was pounded on to rocks in Chale Bay in 1836.

### WHAT TO LOOK OUT FOR

The massive landslides around St Catherine's Point have created a undercliff world rich in wildlife. The tumbled land of hummocks and hollows with temporary ponds are the first landfall for migratory butterflies. It is also one of the best places to watch migrating birds in spring.

# Tennyson's Freshwater

*From lofty downland with magnificent coastal views to tranquil estuary scenes, this exhilarating ramble explores the landscape the Romantic poet loved so well.*

**DISTANCE** *5.75 miles (9.2km)* **MINIMUM TIME** *3hrs*

**ASCENT/GRADIENT** *623ft (190m)* ▲▲▲ **LEVEL OF DIFFICULTY** +++

**PATHS** *Downland, field and woodland paths, some road walking and stretch of disused railway, 4 stiles*

**LANDSCAPE** *Downland, farmland, freshwater marsh and salt marsh*

**SUGGESTED MAP** *OS Explorer OL29 Isle of Wight*

**START / FINISH** *Grid reference: SZ 346857*

**DOG FRIENDLINESS** *Let off lead on Tennyson Down and along old railway*

**PARKING** *Pay-and-display car park at Freshwater Bay*

**PUBLIC TOILETS** *Freshwater Bay and Yarmouth*

Away from the bustle of the resort towns, West Wight is a quieter, less populated area of great natural beauty, offering areas of open countryside, rugged cliffs, wonderful views and a fascinating wildlife. This exhilarating ramble encapsulates the contrasting landscapes of the area, from the wildlife-rich tidal estuary of the River Yar to magnificent chalk headlands and hills with their breathtaking views.

## Solitary Walks

Of the many literary greats who sought seclusion and inspiration on the island during the 19th century, it was the poet Alfred, Lord Tennyson who chose to reside in West Wight. Tennyson and his wife Emily first came to Farringford House, a castellated late-Georgian house (now a hotel) set in parkland beneath Tennyson Down, in 1853. From the drawing room he could look out across Freshwater Bay and the slopes of Afton Down, a view he believed to be the most beautiful in England – 'Mediterranean in its richness and charm'. Almost daily he would take long solitary walks across the chalk downland, enjoying the bracing air, which he declared to be 'worth sixpence a pint'. The island inspired some of his greatest poems. *The Charge of the Light Brigade* was written on the Down that now bears his name, and *Maud*, *Enoch Arden* and the *Idylls of the King* at Farringford.

Tennyson's poetry was so popular that he soon became one of the richest poets in the country. Combined with his magnetic genius and personality, he soon changed the face of West Wight, as tiny Freshwater became the cultural centre of England, attracting the most eminent Victorians of his age – Charles Kingsley, Garibaldi, Lewis Carroll, Charles Darwin, Prince Albert – to name but a few. Farringford was the perfect place to entertain friends and celebrities, despite or because of its remoteness, but it was his time spent alone wandering the Downs or with his wife Emily in their fine garden that made Farringford so special. They bought a house on the mainland and only returned to Farringford for the winter, when they would be undisturbed. Alfred died in 1892 and Emily nearly four years later in 1896.

Memories of the great man and his family are dotted along this walk. On Tennyson Down, you will find the granite monument erected in his honour in 1897. On quieter days you can imagine the poet striding up the hill, dressed in his flowing Spanish cloak, wide-brimmed hat and stout holly stick, for his favourite downland walk. You can take lunch or afternoon tea at Farringford Hotel. In Freshwater, step inside All Saints Church to view the memorials to the family, while in the peaceful churchyard you will find Emily's grave and a lovely view across the serene estuary of the River Yar.

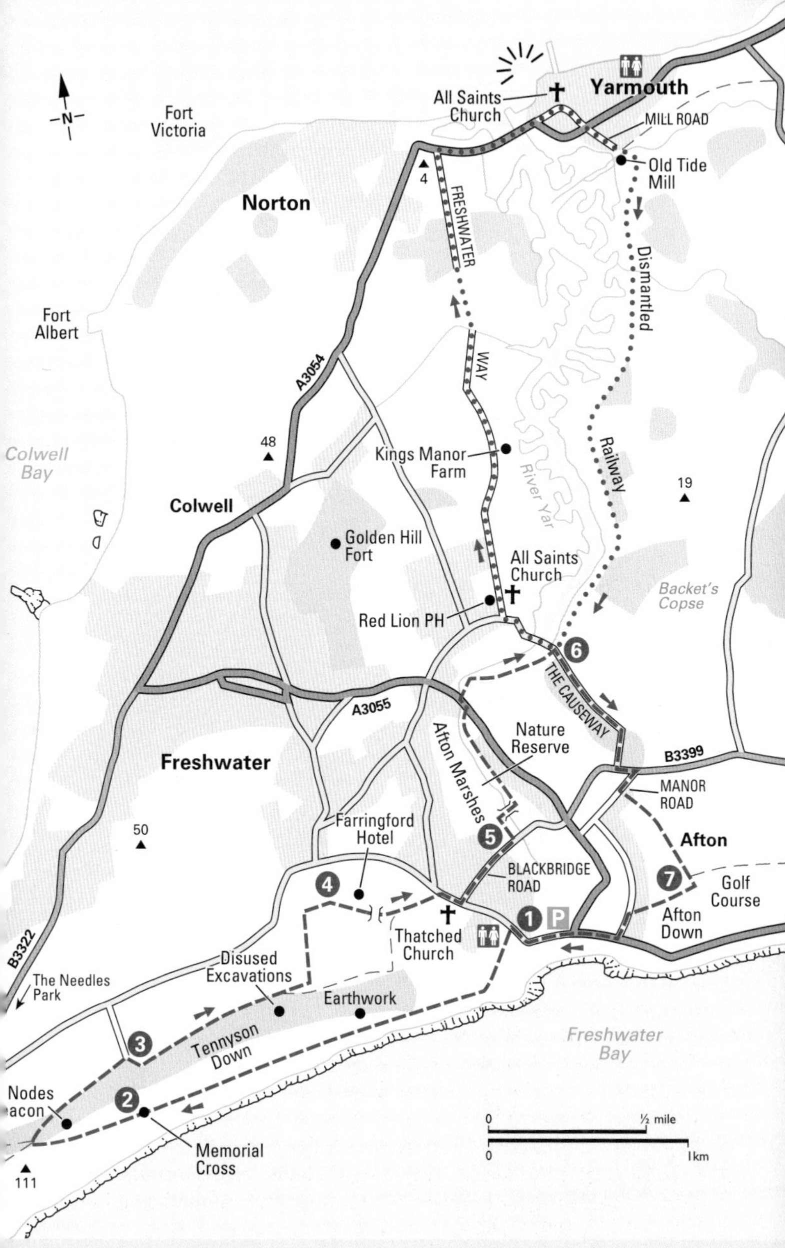


Overleaf: Freshwater Bay (Walks 48 & 49)

## WALK 48 DIRECTIONS

1 From the car park, turn right along the road, then left before the bus shelter along a metalled track, signed 'Coastal Path'. After 50yds (46m) bear right through a gate and follow the well-walked path through a gateway and up to the memorial cross at the summit of Tennyson Down.

2 Continue down the wide grassy swathe, which narrows between gorse bushes, to reach the replica of the Old Nodes Beacon. Here, turn very sharp right down a chalk track. At a junction (car park right) keep straight on up the narrow path.

3 The path widens, then descends to a gate into woodland. Proceed close to the woodland fringe before emerging into more open countryside. Just beyond a disused pit on your right, fork left at a waymark post down a narrower path. Cross a stile, then follow the enclosed path as it turns sharp left to a stile. Cross the next field to a stile and turn right along the field-edge to a stile.

4 Cross a farm track, go through a gate and walk along the track (F47) beside Farringford Hotel. Pass beneath a wooden footbridge and continue downhill to a gate and the road. (Turn left if you wish to visit the hotel). Turn right; then, opposite the thatched church, turn left down Blackbridge Road. Just before Black Bridge, turn left into Afton Marshes Nature Reserve.

5 Join the nature trail, following it across a footbridge and beside the stream to the A3055 (this can be very wet in winter). Turn left and almost immediately cross over to join bridleway (F61) along the course of the old railway. In 0.5 mile (800m) reach the Causeway. Turn left here for the longer loop of Walk 49 or to visit Freshwater church and the Red Lion.

6 On this shorter walk turn right and continue to the B3399. Turn left and shortly cross on to unmetalled Manor Road. In a few paces, bear left , signed 'Freshwater Way', and ascend across grassland towards Afton Down.

7 Keep ahead at a junction of paths beside the golf course, soon to follow the gravel track right to the clubhouse. Go through a gate, pass in front of the building to reach the access track, keeping left to the A3055. Turn right downhill into Freshwater Bay.

### WHILE YOU'RE THERE

Visit the Needles Park at Alum Bay. Take the spectacular chairlift to the beach to view the strange multi-coloured sands for which it is famous, take a boat trip to view the Needles at close quarters, and explore the restored Old Battery, built in 1862, with its viewing platform and exhibition of the history of the headland.

### WHAT TO LOOK OUT FOR

As you walk through the reedbeds and scrub of Afton Marsh Nature Reserve, look out for kingfishers and the yellow blooms of the marsh marigold, among many other birds and marsh plants that thrive there. On Tennyson Down you may see rare chalk-loving flowers and grasses, including bee orchids and nettle-leaved bellflowers, and hundred of small butterflies, such as common, chalkhill, small and Adonis blues, skippers and dark green fritillaries.

# Yarmouth and the Yar Valley

*A longer loop takes you out by the marshes of the Yar Valley to Yarmouth.*

**See map and information panel for Walk 48**



DISTANCE *9.5 miles (15.3km)* MINIMUM TIME *4hrs 30min*

ASCENT/GRADIENT *738ft (225m)* ▲▲▲ LEVEL OF DIFFICULTY +++

## WALK 49 DIRECTIONS (Walk 48 option)

On reaching the Causeway after Point 5 on Walk 48, turn left and follow the lane to All Saints Church and the Red Lion in Freshwater. Take the waymarked path (Freshwater Way) between a cottage and the churchyard wall. Cross a stile and continue along the farm road. At the farmyard entrance cross the double stile on the left and bear right along the field-edge to a stile. Go through a kissing gate at the entrance to Kings Manor Farm, and follow the signposted Freshwater Way along a wide track to a gate and junction of paths. Climb the stile on the right, pass through a copse and bear left, uphill, along the field-edge. Enter the field on your left and walk along the right-hand edge to a stile. Drop down through woodland, turn left along a track to reach the A3054. Turn right and cross the bridge into Yarmouth, bearing left at the roundabout into the town centre.

With its stone quays, old houses and harbour, you will find Yarmouth a lively, interesting and picturesque little town. Stroll through the town square, walk to the end of the pier for superb views across the Solent, and enjoy some well earned refreshment in one of the numerous tea rooms and pubs, before heading back to Freshwater.

From the Square, head for the church and walk along St James Street. Cross the A3054 into Mill Road, then at the sharp left bend, keep ahead towards the old tide mill, built in 1793 to harness the tidal flow of the estuary. Walk by the mudflats and turn right along the old railway line, following it for 1.5 miles (2.4km) to the Causeway. Turn left to rejoin Walk 48 at Point 6.

Birdlife abounds on the expanse of saltings and mudflats of the Yar Estuary at low tide. As well as the common waders, look out for the curlew probing the mudflats, the bright red legs of the redshank, and, in winter, the flocks of brent geese feeding in neighbouring fields. The thickets along the old railway track are a haven to cuckoos and nightingales.

### WHERE TO EAT AND DRINK

Freshwater Bay has a pub and tea rooms (closed Wednesdays and Thursdays). Lunch and afternoon teas can be found at Farringford Hotel. Good pub food is available at the Red Lion in Freshwater, while Yarmouth offers a choice of pubs, restaurants and cafés.

# Nature Reserve and Ancient Borough

*Discover the history of the island's former capital and birdlife on the salt marshes and creeks of the Newtown Etuary.*

**DISTANCE** *3.5 miles (5.6km)* **MINIMUM TIME** *2hrs*
**ASCENT/GRADIENT** *85ft (25m)* ▲▲▲ **LEVEL OF DIFFICULTY** +++
**PATHS** *Tracks, field paths, raised dykes and some roads, 2stiles*
**LANDSCAPE** *Gently rolling farmland, woodland and salt marsh*
**SUGGESTED MAP** *OS Explorer OL 29 Isle of Wight*
**START / FINISH** *Grid reference: SZ 413894*
**DOG FRIENDLINESS** *Keep dogs under control*
**PARKING** *Shalfleet village car park, off A3054*
**PUBLIC TOILETS** *NT toilets in Old Town Hall car park; donation appreciated*

## WALK 50 DIRECTIONS

Shalfleet developed where the Caul Bourne widens into a creek at the head of the Newtown Estuary. Take a look at the church with its impressive, fort-like tower, built in the 11th century with 5ft (1.5m) thick walls and used as a refuge from French invaders during the 14th century, and stroll out to the small 17th-century quay, once busy with boats unloading coal or taking on corn and now popular with yachts and sailing dinghies.

Turn left out of the car park, then right at the fork down Mill Road to pass Shalfleet Mill. Cross the footbridge and follow the path up through woodland to a metalled drive. Bear left and follow the drive to a road. Turn left and keep to the road for 200yds (183m) to a gate and permissive path on your left. Keep to the right-hand edge of two fields, parallel with the road, to a gate. Turn left, then left again along Town Lane, signed to Newtown. Cross the bridge at the head of Causeway Lake and take the path left, towards Newtown village. Walk along the edge of the tidal creek to a gate, then along the edge of Hay Meadow. Keep to the path as it bears right to a gate to join a tree-lined path leading into Newtown.

The most ancient of the island boroughs, Francheville, as Newtown was once known, was the island's capital, being laid out by the Bishop of Winchester in 1256. Situated on the Newtown River estuary, it developed into a major seaport, with great, masted ships dwarfing bustling quays and trade thriving with local salt and

### WHILE YOU'RE THERE

Visit Newtown Old Town Hall. This small, brick and stone building was built in the 17th century and stands as a monument to Newtown's past eminence. It houses an exhibition depicting the famous Ferguson's Gang who restored the building before giving it to the National Trust, and a copy of ancient documents of this notorious 'Rotten' Borough.

**WHAT TO LOOK OUT FOR**

Note the finely painted board or inn sign, featuring the arms of the former borough, above the doorway to a fine stone house called Noah's Ark in Newtown. Formerly the village inn, it is the village's oldest surviving building and surrendered its licence in 1916.

oysters. Its streets were designed on a grid system and their names recall the medieval merchants and craftsmen – Gold Street, Drapers Alley – although most are now only grassy lanes. All this changed in 1377 when the town was burnt down by a combined French and Spanish raid. It was never fully rebuilt, although the town hall was rebuilt in 1699 and until 1832 it returned two Members of Parliament.

Today, Newtown, which has no through traffic, is a tranquil place and best explored on foot. You can wander along a network of footpaths through the old streets and visit the beautifully restored Victorian church, and the isolated town hall where you can learn more about the history of this fascinating place.

At the lane, keep ahead and follow it left to pass a parking area. Take the path through a gate beside the Old Coastguard Station. Beyond a further gate, keep to the left-hand edge of the meadow to a gate and follow the raised path alongside the estuary.

Perhaps surprisingly, the windswept salt marshes and mudflats were only created in their present form as late as 1954, following a violent winter storm which breached the sea wall. Bordering shallow creeks and the estuary, it is a magical place, and a paradise for both birds and birders. Wildfowl and waders abound here. Oystercatchers and redshanks probe the mudflats for morsels, a variety of ducks dabble in the shallows, nesting gulls squabble on Gull Island, and common and little terns gracefully glide through the shimmering summer air, while flocks of geese wheel overhead in winter, and always and everywhere you will hear the evocative bubbling call of the curlew. For a small fee you can visit the bird reserve and watch from well positioned hides.

Continue to the sheds at Newtown Quay, then head inland across the narrow wooden boardwalk to a gate. In a few paces turn left and follow the footpath towards the bird hide. Bear right at a gate, heading inland to a drive and the lane. Turn left, cross the stile on your left and proceed behind the houses to a stile and lane. Turn right, pass the old town hall and follow the lane down to the bridge at Causeway Lake. From here retrace your steps back to Shalfleet Mill and the car park. An enjoyable extra mile (1.6km) can be added by following the footpath you'll see right at the end of Mill Road. Walk along the track parallel with the tidal Shalfleet Lake to Shalfleet Quay for a different view of Newtown River and its tidal creeks.

**WHERE TO EAT AND DRINK**

The welcoming, 18th-century New Inn at Shalfleet boasts flagstoned floors, a huge open fireplace, scrubbed pine tables, a good range of ales, and an interesting menu that specialises in fresh local fish. There's also a sheltered rear garden.

# Walking in Safety

All these walks are suitable for any reasonably fit person, but less experienced walkers should try the easier walks first. Route finding is usually straightforward, but you will find that an Ordnance Survey map is a useful addition to the route maps and descriptions.

## RISKS

Although each walk here has been researched with a view to minimising the risks to the walkers who follow its route, no walk in the countryside can be considered to be completely free from risk. Walking in the outdoors will always require a degree of common sense and judgement to ensure that it is as safe as possible.

- Be particularly careful on cliff paths and in upland terrain, where the consequences of a slip can be very serious.
- Remember to check tidal conditions before walking on the seashore.
- Some sections of route are by, or cross, busy roads. Take care and remember traffic is a danger even on minor country lanes.
- Be careful around farmyard machinery and livestock, especially if you have children with you.
- Be aware of the consequences of changes in the weather and check the forecast before you set out. Carry spare clothing and a torch if you are walking in the winter months. Remember the weather can change very quickly at any time of the year, and in moorland and heathland areas, mist and fog can make route finding much harder. Don't set out in these conditions unless you are confident of your navigation skills in poor visibility. In summer remember to take account of the heat and sun; wear a hat and carry spare water.
- On walks away from centres of population you should carry a whistle and survival bag. If you do have an accident requiring the emergency services, make a note of your position as accurately as possible and dial 999.

## COUNTRYSIDE CODE

- Be safe, plan ahead and follow any signs.
- Leave gates and property as you find them.
- Protect plants and animals and take your litter home.
- Keep dogs under close control.
- Consider other people.

For more information visit www.naturalengland.org.uk/ourwork/enjoying/countrysidecode